The Secre
of an Airport
Airside – A Look Behind the Scenes

MARTYN CARTLEDGE

Front cover image: Aerial view of Seoul Incheon Airport.

Back cover image: Emirates A380 being turned around at Manchester Airport, UK.

Title page image: Aerial view of Hamad International Airport, Doha Qatar.

Contents page image: Stands and runways of Seoul Incheon Airport.

To my wife and taxi driver Sheena, who is often left behind when I travel the world.
Cornwall will always be a talking point…

Published by Key Books
An imprint of Key Publishing Ltd
PO Box 100
Stamford
Lincs PE9 1XQ

www.keypublishing.com

The right of Martyn Cartledge to be identified as the author of this book has been asserted in accordance with the Copyright, Designs and Patents Act 1988 Sections 77 and 78.

Copyright © Martyn Cartledge, 2023

ISBN 978 1 80282 508 4

All rights reserved. Reproduction in whole or in part in any form whatsoever or by any means is strictly prohibited without the prior permission of the Publisher.

Typeset by SJmagic DESIGN SERVICES, India.

Contents

Foreword

Airports are fascinating places from which you 'fly away' to far away destinations to experience different cultures. Each airport aims to be a simple, secure, technological, and ever-more sustainable, with a touch of 'sense of place'. By unveiling the 'behind the scenes', you, the reader, will have the opportunity to appreciate the complex system of an airport.

This book, written by a great expert in air transport and experienced photographer, describes how the passion and professional skills of airport workers, under the guidance of a competent organisation, are fundamental to managing the complexities of the day-to-day running of an airport.

The passenger journey should be simple and smooth, from arrival in the terminal to the boarding gate. Behind the terminal area, often invisible to passengers, lies the most complex part of the airport, 'Airside', where activities are managed with a 'safety first' approach to all ground operations. The process is constantly monitored from arrival to take-off. Arriving passengers and luggage are transferred to the terminal, while those departing are conveyed to the boarding gate. All these activities are simultaneous: routine technical checks are performed, the aircraft is refuelled, the cabin is cleaned, and luggage is boarded. All these processes are overseen by stakeholders, who in turn address issues and attempt to increase the number of on-time departures.

Airports are increasingly obliged to play a crucial role in environmental sustainability, facing the transition to Zero Emission processes by introducing different methods to ensure energy efficiency, renewable resources, and sustainable fuels.

Martyn helps to discover the hidden face of the airport. Giving the passenger the opportunity to peek behind the closed doors makes, in my opinion, the flight experience even more amazing. Furthermore, he keeps us entertained with the addition of some odd and amusing incidents on the way!

Alessandro Fidato
Chief Operating Officer
SEA Milan Airports

Introduction

What comes to mind when you think of an airport? Holidays, business, noise even?

The sheer size of many, small towns in themselves, once prompted an airport's operations director to suggest to me that airports could actually be described as an ecosystem, given all the intertwined departments relying on one another to complete the core operation of getting aircraft and its passengers in and out safely, which I thought was very apt.

Why on earth are there so many buildings when we passengers only use the big one at the front, without even catching a glimpse inside any of the others? What do all the people who work there actually do? There are many different departments and roles at an airport, indeed far too many to go into them all in detail in just one book.

Just what is 'Airside' anyway? Although official dictionary definitions do vary somewhat, Airside is, in essence, any area of an airport or airfield that to access would require some form of security checks. This includes any areas where aircraft are manoeuvring or where they might be accessed, and also what passengers might call the departure lounge, the place where we are once we have gone through security.

Looking over the ramp at Manchester Airport.

Chapter 1

Airport Ops

The airport operations (Ops) department is at the very core of the running of an airport. This is not to denigrate all the other very important departments that an airport cannot do without, it is simply that these people keep the airport functioning and are the very strands of DNA that hold things together. It is sadly not within the scope of this book to list every job and role that makes up an airport, however, this is not to say that they are unimportant. I have endeavoured to go through what I feel are the main and/or most interesting areas. Just who belongs in the operations department will differ at each airport, so for sake of ease I am including anybody who works directly to keep the airport running.

On top of the operational pile is the airfield duty manager, or ADM, who, if not in direct charge of all the other people working on the airfield, is broadly responsible for them. In fact, an airfield cannot be certified unless it has an ADM. No certification equals no flights. One ADM told me that everything that happens on the airfield is his responsibility. 'It's down to me', he said! Another had an altogether different take on this. 'It's my airfield. I can do what I want here', he said, whilst taking a shortcut over the grass to stop on a taxiway, thereby blocking the path of an oncoming Air Jamaica A300 so I could take a photo.

The ADM also attends any incident or major works on the airfield and will already have had a meeting with Air Traffic Control (ATC), the airport Rescue and Fire Fighting Services (RFFS), security and any major contractors on site. Major incidents are, thankfully, rare at airports, but one

Airfield duty manager's (ADM) vehicle.

The Air Jamaica A300 that was blocked by a Miami ADM.

ADM did recount a flavour of what is dealt with. He recalled that sometimes it is simple incidents such as a twisted ankle from stepping in a small hole in the apron, which would require filling as soon as possible. However, more dramatic occurrences can also occur, such as the time this particular ADM dragged a man out of a cloud of vaporised hydraulic fluid, or a serious incident when an aircraft tyre blew out whilst undergoing maintenance, leaving the engineer with very serious injuries and the aircraft unusable for a couple of days due to damage and the subsequent enquiries. There was also the diversion of an L1011 inbound to Brize Norton from Afghanistan, which became rather complicated due to the aircraft having active service personnel with live munitions on board. On a different side of the scale, this ADM told me a story of a group of people whose equipment is a lot less dangerous (depending on how you see the standard dress sense of the average footballer): he was asked to arrange for the England football team to have an apron transfer to avoid the crowds building inside. It's just a shame one speedy footballer wasn't around when a greyhound escaped from a container being loaded onto an aircraft, as they could have been some help to the agile staff members who resolved it!

ADM marking a section of defective ramp.

Over 20 years ago, in Italy, another ADM shares a dog story that is something out of a

A Lufthansa CRJ-200 cordoned off after an incident.

An RAF L1011 disgorging armed service personnel.

theatre farce. Baggage handlers alerted airfield Ops that a dog had been found dead in its crate in the hold. Now, it just so happened that, roaming free around the airport, there was a dog with an uncannily similar appearance to the deceased version in the aircraft hold. So, the dead dog was replaced with the airport stray, only for the owner to be totally overwhelmed when reunited. The problem being, the owner's dog was already dead when it entered the hold and was merely being transported home!

The primary role of all the Ops team, however, is keeping the airfield safe whilst maintaining the greatest efficiency, with the ADM having oversight. The ADM and other Ops staff will be mobile in highly visible vehicles around the runways, taxiways and apron areas checking for issues, defects or simply foreign object debris (FOD), which in essence are bits of rubbish, but, if sucked into an aircraft engine, these can become very expensive and serious pieces of rubbish. It is so ingrained into staff on airfields that, even as a visitor, I now find myself looking for and picking up FOD should I be airside! This might seem not that difficult, but airfields are BIG! London Heathrow's five-square mile footprint has 50 miles of taxiways and roads and 448 football pitches' worth of grassed areas.

Every airport must inspect its runways for defects at least twice in every 24 hours and after any runway-involved incident to ensure the runway is still safe to use. Plus, a runway lighting inspection must be undertaken each night. These inspections also provide Air Taffic Control (ATC) with the official braking action expected for the runway. This is then passed onto the crews of landing aircraft. However, in some areas of the world, there can be some quite specific issues. Runways are, more often than not, grooved to help friction, and these grooves can slowly fill up with rubber deposited from landing aircraft, requiring removal every so often, generally by high-pressure water jets. All runways, grooved or not, will have some level of rubber build up. In areas such as the Middle East, the high temperatures increase rubber deposits, which means the time between cleaning could be reduced to just two week intervals. It is not only rubber that the Middle East has a problem in

ADM in discussion over airfield repairs.

ADM vehicle on the runway at night

The touchdown point at the Greek Island of Skiathos, which is famed for its short and narrow runway.

regard to grooved runways: sand is also a problem. In response to this, a different compound is now used to coat the runway that does not require grooves. It is just as important to ensure the grooves are correctly made, as Bristol Airport found when it had to close because of a number of airlines boycotting the airport following multiple runway excursions in a day because of grooving issues. Minor defects in the taxiway and apron surfaces can be repaired temporarily with what has been described to me as 'hot pour'. However, this has to be used sparingly and only on small defects. I know of an issue where a much larger area was repaired, but which spectacularly backfired when a Saab 340 actually got stuck in the repaired section, requiring the deplaning of passengers to get the aircraft free.

Ops staff will also drive 'Follow Me' vehicles, which are used regularly by some airports but less so by others. The role of these vehicles is self-explanatory, as it is a ground vehicle that guides an aircraft around the airfield, generally with a rearward-facing sign on the vehicle stating 'Follow Me'. ATC will also have instructed the crew to follow the vehicle. Not all airports use these vehicles all the time: they may be used for aircrew who are unsure of the airport's layout and need assistance; the green taxiway lights may be inoperative; or it may be that the airport has a specific requirement, such as the direction of government aircraft. In most cases, these vehicles are similar to the other general airport Ops vehicles. There are one or two exceptions, often to do with sponsorship or a promotion of some kind. Zeltweg Air Base in Austria has used a Smart car in the past, with Bologna Guglielmo Marconi Airport in Italy jumping to the other end of the scale and operating a Lamborghini. However, Hannover Airport in Germany is possibly the biggest proponent in the use of sporty vehicles in this role. It has used a Mini Cooper and a Porsche Cayman, with the most recent addition being an Audi R8, which it claims is the fastest Follow Me car in the world. Not sure Bologna would agree with that, however!

Hannover's sporty
Follow Me vehicles.

Aircraft follow the green centrelights whilst taxiing to their allotted stand.

Zeltweg's Follow Me Smart car. (Gerhard66, public domain, via Wikimedia Commons)

A Frankfurt Follow Me vehicle leading a Cathay Pacific 747.

At smaller airports or at stands that do not have the self-parking technology discussed later, then it is down to an Ops person with a couple of brightly coloured bats or light sticks, at night, to use specific signals to guide the flight crew in, bringing the aircraft into position based on the markings on the apron, which show aircraft types.

Then there are the more seemingly mundane jobs which can be as simple as keeping doors opening or gutters cleaned, or the more specific roles such as

Marshaller showing the 'Stop' command with light sticks.

Above left: Marshaller guiding a Ryanair 737 into its correct position at Bergamo Airport, near Milan.

Above right: Cherry picker used for maintenance on terminal buildings.

Below: Night scene showing the many lights on an airfield.

View of runway approach lights with an easyJet A320 lining up in the background.

maintaining airfield lighting. Just look out over an airfield the next time you are in a terminal at night, and you will see just how big a job that is likely to be. The scene is almost Christmas-like, with lights of many different colours spread as far as you can see. From the approach lights guiding aircraft onto the runways to the gate area including taxiways and signage, airports often have a dedicated team looking after the Aeronautical Ground Lighting, which at a major airport comprises many thousands of fittings (runway/taxiway/approach/signage/obstruction lighting) requiring inspection and maintenance every 24 hours to ensure the airport is compliant with international standards. The team is also responsible for associated equipment such as high mast lighting and streetlighting (airfield and front of house), runway friction assessments, and general electrical issues. Ops also look after fixed electrical ground power and Advanced Visual Docking Guidance systems, both on a planned and reactive basis. There is the old joke about how many people it takes to change a bulb, and for airports, it's pretty much a one-man operation. It's a relatively simple process to change a fitting once any required arrangements have been made. The bolts holding the unit in place are removed first, the unit is then levered out to expose the simple push/pull electrical connection. The opposite is then done to the replacement, with the torque wrench providing the correct amount of tightness to the securing bolts.

One job that will only have dedicated teams at airports regularly affected is that of snow clearance. At most airfields snow clearance duties are a secondary role to Ops staff and one that will be called upon as and when is necessary. The ADM is, again, front and centre of any decisions made when snow and ice are either forecast or present. Years of experience comes in handy to judge what to do with regard to

An easyJet A320 taking off from Faro Airport, Portugal, with runway approach lights in the foreground.

Above: Sunken LED airfield light.

Left: It only takes one airfield operations person to change a light bulb!

Below: ADM vehicle in the snow.

a forecast, as the use of anti-icing fluids is an important and potentially expensive decision. To anti-ice an airfield costs many thousands of pounds and if it is put down at the wrong time, it could either be washed away or simply ineffective. However, get it right and you have a situation where you reap the rewards of being open for business when all around you are closed.

Snow clearance is quite a precise, choreographed job, with the ploughs and brushes working in a staggered way that ensures the snow is moved from the centre of the runways bit by bit to the side by means of pushing it from one plough to the next, with the last in line actually moving it off the runway completely. Even then, the job may not be over because if these banks of snow get too high, they could become a danger to aircraft on the runway. In this case, they are either dispersed by means of snow blowing equipment or are moved to pre-ordained snow dump areas.

One other role OPS often attend to is that of bird scaring. However, there are so many ways of doing this that it deserves a chapter all of its own.

Anti-icing vehicle operating on a runway.

Snow clearance machines performing a well-choreographed operation on the runway.

Chapter 2

Bird Scaring

O ne of the great ironies of modern flight is the vulnerability to those creatures whose natural domain is the sky: birds. 'Bird strikes', the name given to the event where an airborne aircraft comes into contact with one or more birds, are surprisingly common. In fact, the Federal Aviation Administration (FAA) logs more than 10,000 a year. Bird vs plane collisions can result in minor damage to aircraft such as simple exterior dents. However, encounters with flocks or perhaps a single large bird can severely damage an aircraft, particularly if ingested into one or more of the engines, causing partial or even full loss of thrust. Just ask Capt Chesley 'Sully' Sullenberger, as it was a bird strike that led to him and his co-pilot, Jeff Skiles, performing the 'Miracle on the Hudson'. This involved US Airways flight 1549, which, while climbing through 2,800ft, struck a flock of geese four minutes after take-off, subsequently losing thrust in both engines leading to a landing in New York's Hudson River.

Airports employ a vast range of devices and techniques to scare away birds, as a bird strike at the critical phases of take-off and landing, a height where greater numbers of birds are found, can be very serious indeed. The most visible of these are Ops staff firing shells into the air, creating a loud bang aimed at moving the birds on. Birds can be much smarter than we might initially think. This type of single bang can become something they grow accustomed to, so other types of munitions and the way they are used have been introduced with multiple shots being fired. At some airports, I have seen gas-fired cannons, which produce a loud bang. Although at one Portuguese airport I was told that they are no longer used there as the birds have been known to not only ignore the noise, but actually sit in the cannons and not move even when they fire! Another well-used and effective method is to broadcast the distress call of the relative species, thus fooling the birds into thinking there are predators in the vicinity.

Some airports have taken the predator idea to the ultimate. In what seems a rather counterintuitive plan, it is not that uncommon to find airports with falconry centres. I visited a couple in my travels at Ibiza and Faro. The Faro facility is situated on a hill overlooking the main runway threshold and houses 20 birds. These are not any old birds, these are perfect hunting machines that are flown regularly. Their potential prey know this and keep a wide berth, particularly when flying – perfect for a busy runway. This type of facility often forms part of a larger environmental management system, integrated into the overall airport management. AENA, the world's leading airport operator in terms of passenger numbers, manages 46 airports and two heliports in Spain, including Ibiza, takes this view.

Aftermath of a heron vs jet engine collision. (Paolo Perego)

Right: A gas-powered cannon designed to scare off birds.

Below: A Faro-based bird of prey overlooking its airport.

The falconry centre (Halconera) at Ibiza.

Like all AENA airports, Ibiza also has a falconry centre as a means of bird control. Considered to be amongst the most effective means of bird control, the centre is tucked away at the rear of the fire station and has a variety of different birds of prey that are regularly flown. Permission to practice falconry is renewed on a yearly basis.

Conversely, should the problem be these or other birds of prey, different methods are employed. In the USA, the US Department of Agriculture has a team of wildlife experts, which are often on-site at airports to identify, track, safely trap, and relocate such birds many miles from the airport environment, including flightpaths in and out. There are some even more ingenious (or wacky) ideas out there. In the USA, Salt Lake City uses pigs to predate on gull eggs, with border collies giving chase to egrets and herons at Fort Myers Airport.

Technology is also increasingly used to combat the threat. In France, a test at Tarbes-Lourdes-Pyrénées Airport used LED screens to display a graphic that was described as 'looming eyes' to scare off raptors and corvids in the area. Radar systems are used at some airports, including Seattle-Tacoma, Amsterdam and Istanbul, not only to direct aircraft but also to monitor the size, location and movements of flocks within a set distance around the airport. This allows controllers to activate air cannons, time the arrivals or departures of flights to avoid large flocks, and even dispatch staff to use

A British Airways 747 surrounded by a flock of birds.

lethal methods to control the bird situation in an area. The system also allows pilots as well as ground crew to report wildlife to airport operations teams.

Although not a major issue for commercial airliners, birds can also cause problems to aircraft inside hangars, where birds will perch and poop on planes. As anybody who has been left a bird poop on their car for more than a few days will testify, bird excrement is highly corrosive and can erode an aircraft's exterior. Realistic figurines of predators in the buildings can offer a good deterrent, but high-tech alternatives are also in use here, with machines circulating aromas that repel birds, as is the case at Chicago-O'Hare, where, apparently, pigeons hate the smell of grapes!

Airports would prefer not to have to scare birds away and try very hard to deter birds in the first place, often altering the on-site and nearby landscape to be less bird friendly. In fact, I was once told of an airport that had a relatively sudden increase in bird strikes. The airport initially, rather oddly, thought it was because of an airline logo containing a bird. It eventually turned out to be a leaking pipe creating a difficult to see small pond in an otherwise very dry area, attracting the birds to it. If you see the grass being mown, this is not to keep the airport looking smart, it is done to a height that will deter birds from loitering in the area. Habitat features, including open areas of grass and water as well as shrubs and trees, can provide food and roosting sites for birds. These are often modified to become less attractive to birds. Some airports go even further by replacing grass with gravel.

Oh, and staff also shout at them too!

Chapter 3

Apron Control

Many jobs at an airport come with a view, but not many beat apron control. The very essence of the job is all about the airfield's parking stands and a view of them is essential. Therefore, the view out of the office windows is generally pretty spectacular, and eyesight is often backed up by CCTV. ATC can, of course, have the same view but only if you work in the Visual Control Room (VCR).

When not taking in the view, just what does an apron or airfield controller do? At the very basic level, it is deciding where an aircraft will park. That said, it is not like parking a car, where you would simply find the nearest spot. The process requires considerable planning, which will firstly be seasonal, and then three or four weeks before the day that plan is further tweaked with any changes. A final plan will then be created the day before the flight's arrival. There are so many different factors to be considered when it comes to which stand an aircraft is allocated. It is like a massive game of Tetris. First off, it must be at the correct terminal at airports with more than one. Then there is MARS. No, not the planet, but an acronym for Multi Aircraft Ramp System. This is a system whereby each stand will be made up of a left, right and centre position. If a wide-body aircraft is to be parked in it would be on its own in the centre position. However, each of the left and right positions can accommodate narrow-body aircraft side by side, so you don't want to put a single narrow body aircraft there if there are no wide-bodied stands left.

Furthermore, airlines might have their own requirements or have requested preferred stands to operate their services from. The most regular issue though, is to do with aircraft arriving early or late,

The view from apron control at Naples International Airport.

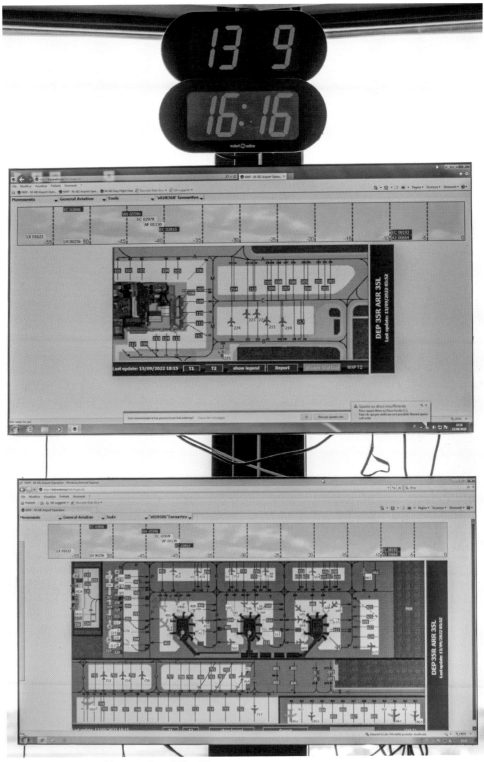

Screens showing parking stands at Milan Linate.

An Emirates A380 seen from Apron Control.

alongside late departures and maintenance issues, making a stand unavailable. One option that has started to be used for aircraft ready to depart, but without an airborne slot to match, is to push away from the stand and then park elsewhere. The use of this depends on the expected wait time, which, if long, means significant fuel burn, unless you stop then later self-start your engines. This method means that stands become available, with the added benefit that the airline and airport can list the flight as an 'on time departure' despite sitting around for ages after push back!

Other methods can be almost clandestine in their nature. At one major airport, the now-defunct airline bmi always used the same stand for a regular, flight destination. However, on one particular day, the inbound aircraft encountered an issue and was in need of maintenance and would depart empty, instead of with its passengers, who now were to be booked on other flights, but, by this time, were already at the gate. Not wanting these passengers to see the aircraft arrive seemingly fine but depart without them, the airline requested apron control use a stand away from sight of passengers to hide the aircraft. Without being David Copperfield, making a full size airliner disappear was not the easiest task!

Sometimes, there are simply not enough stands with direct access to the terminal. If this is the case, aircraft must then be parked, as per the plan, on what are called 'remote stands' and bussed to the terminal. Part of an airfield controller's role is to minimise the use of remote stands, as they are not anyone's preferred position! In fact, if you have ever sat on an aircraft after landing, waiting to park wondering why the aircraft is not using any of the empty stands you can see out of the window, it might well be that your allocated stand is pre-allocated. Those stands may well have aircraft due on them soon, and changing their usage plan for the day would cause a domino effect of more issues later on. You may think that it would be easier and quicker to park on a remote stand? Not so, as the busses may already be allocated to those aircraft planned to be there. All it could achieve would be to change the view out of the window with the wait time still the same, or perhaps even worse!

A typical shift for an airfield controller would involve both planning for the following day and dealing with the issues that crop up, putting them at, what I once heard called, the 'very pointy end of the sharpest stick'! So, next time you are sitting on an aircraft waiting for it to park and let you off, just remember, it's not being done for fun – apron control are just as keen to get you off as you are.

Geneva Airport apron control as seen from the ramp.

Chapter 4

Airport Rescue and Fire-Fighting Services

O ne could assume Airport fire fighters spend their days drinking tea, playing snooker and watching TV behind those big red doors, right? This image couldn't be more wrong, as I found out from my visits to different services around the world. There is a great deal more to being an airport fire-fighter than you might initially assume. As one told me, 'its very rare that we get a shout which involves squirting water at airplanes, that is just a small part of what we are here for'.

What are they there for? And what determines the structure of the service, the type of equipment and staffing levels? There are statutory requirements set down that determine the staffing requirements and procedures of airport Rescue and Fire-Fighting Services (RFFS). Condition 2 of the Aerodrome Licence requires the airport's licence holder to ensure that RFFS facilities are appropriate to the type of operations. Major airports will often have 'Category 10' status, allowing it to have aircraft such as A380s and 747-8s operating through it. There are a number of different levels below this (although most commercial airlines operate between 7 and 10), each requiring a different number and types of vehicles available, including the staff to operate them. To provide the level of response required, the RFFS rosters its personnel across a watch system that enables cover to be provided during the hours

Fire vehicles are led out on a shout by the Fire Chief.

Above: **Fire tenders at Skiathos.**

Right: **Faro Airport's Rescue and Fire Fighting Services (ARFFS) station.**

of the airport's operation. At major 24/7-operational airfields, each day is often split into two 12-hour shifts. At some airfields, primarily smaller ones, fire cover is maintained by personnel who also hold other job titles.

An airport might have to be closed for a short period when fire-fighters are dealing with a job that then leaves available staff numbers short. I experienced this in mid-2022, when I was at an airport where an A330 had an engine fire on stand. Due to the size of the aircraft, the level of resources that had to be deployed meant that no fire cover was available for any further incidents. This meant an unfortunate ATR 72, on about a two-mile final approach, had to go around and hold until the incident was over. In this incident, the resources slowly came back on stream, meaning that the airport first opened at a lower category before returning to full Category 10.

Emergency cover isn't just provided for aircraft and airfield incidents. Domestic incidents in terminal and office areas on the airfield, and indeed even around the airport complex, can be attended. The issues can be fire-related, but the RFFS also attends medical calls, in which fire-fighters co-respond in partnership with the local ambulance service. It also performs ongoing checks to fire-fighting equipment, such as dry risers in buildings, and conducting post-fire investigations.

When each 12-hour shift changes over, those finishing only leave when their respective colleague arrives, ensuring a full complement of staff should a call out happen during this time. At the beginning of each shift, there is a briefing that details the status of vehicles and the runways/airfield, and each team member is given their role. Operational Advice notes are read out, including any works

Manchester's domestic tender attending a medical call.

Pre-shift watch briefing.

Staff inspect the equipment on a vehicle.

in progress on the airfield that might affect fire service operations, such as the requirement to take a different route to incidents. Additionally, any training drills that are to be run during the shift are discussed. Once the briefing is over, each member of the watch, including the officer in charge, will go about his or her assigned roles, the first of which is to inspect their assigned vehicle and its equipment. Larger airports may also have an incident vehicle to be used as a focal point in times of need.

RFFS vehicles may incorporate standard and infrared cameras as well as an airport-specific sat nav, which, whilst not needed in good daytime weather conditions, has items such as stop bars and the

Above left: The interior of Faro Airport's incident vehicle.

Above right: Firefighters at Faro check the vehicle's monitors.

runway centreline programmed into it, in addition to the road and taxiway system. This is of particular value when the airport is in Low Visibility Procedures (LVP), and becomes invaluable in finding an aircraft in need. There are many different types of RFFS vehicle, with newer versions now equipped with piercing nozzles and multiple monitors (the bits that squirt water, powder or foam to the source of the fire) at the front that can rotate through 190 degrees and reach up to heights of 15m or more. The spray pattern the piercing device emits not only helps put a fire out but importantly will dramatically reduce cabin heat, thereby maintaining a survivable atmosphere. These vehicles are also equipped with high-definition and thermal imaging cameras that enable close-up views of hard-to-reach areas. This means that fire-fighters can remain in the safety of their vehicles for much more of the process, which is a much safer way to operate, although not quite as exciting or dramatic looking!

Left: Infra-red and standard cameras alongside a sat nav in the Fire Chief's vehicle.

Below left: Monitor 'snozzle' piercing an aircraft's skin.

Below right: The spray emitted by a fire-fighting vehicle will dramatically reduce cabin heat, producing a survivable atmosphere.

Above: Close-up of an Oshkosh Striker monitor.

Right: Extinguishing a fire on the training rig.

Fire services with older style vehicles will still employ a mix of vehicle-mounted equipment to deploy water or foam but with a need for firefighters on the ground to approach the fire with hoses and other media.

Some services combine medical and fire services and ambulances are a fairly common sight. There is, at some airfields, equipment that you might not expect to be behind those big doors. For instance, at Faro airport in Portugal, the most interesting vehicles are to be found right at the back. On closer inspection, you will find a small inflatable boat, a quad bike and a Jet Ski, painted in the fire service livery. This airport is surrounded by lagoons, and should anything happen there then these modes of

A fire-fighter externally operates a roof-mounted monitor while others use hand lines.

Fighting a fire this close gets HOT!

Above: **Jet ski and an inflatable boat/ dinghy at Faro.**

Right: **Quad bike at Faro Airport.**

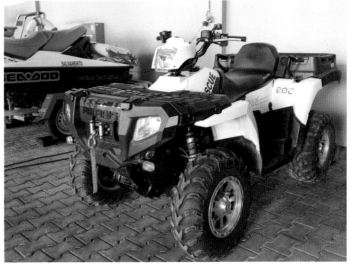

transport enable rapid access to any incident. At Milan Linate, there is a version of the scissor lift vehicle for the deplaning of passengers when all other methods are unavailable.

There may also be some rather special pieces of fire-fighting equipment that, whilst not necessarily part of a particular airport's fire cover, are often parked there for use in the immediate vicinity or locality of the airport. This can include various types of airborne fire-fighting aircraft, necessary if the surrounding area has a greater possibility of wildfires. At Ibiza Airport, for instance, on the BizJet ramp, there is an Air Tractor AT-802, which is operational just for the length of the summer season. On one visit to Pafos Airport, I noticed three Kamov KA 32 helicopters were located adjacent to the fire station. For many years, from 15 May to 15 November, they were positioned in readiness, water scoops attached at the end of a long sling, for their next fire-fighting job, which, on average, was never less than twice a week but could be up to four times a day. At some airports, these types of aircraft will be situated at the 'military side' of the airfield. At Naples International Airport, amongst other governmental departments, the Vigili del Fuoco (Italy's agency for fire and rescue) can be found operating aircraft ranging from the Agusta Bell

A Canadair CL415 water-scooping during fire-fighting duties in Turkey.

An Air Tractor AT-802 on the ramp at Ibiza.

A Kamov KA 32 helicopter with sling-mounted bucket at Paphos, Cyprus.

A Vigili del Fuoco (Italy's agency for fire and rescue) Bell 412 after take-off from Naples.

A Forestale Sikorsky S64F (CH54B) Skycrane on the military ramp at Naples.

Two Bombardier CL-415s on the ground at Naples awaiting their next job.

Exterior of the Vigili del Fuoco station at Milan Malpensa.

412 and Sikorsky CH-54B Tarhe to the amphibious Bombardier CL-415. Milan Malpensa even has its own specialist fire station housing AW109/139s.

At most airfields, there is some form of training facility representing the types of aircraft using the airport to help prepare RFFS members for the issues that they might face on the job. These facilities can be used to mimic cabin evacuation or, when the technology is present, to recreate fires in various parts of the aircraft. I have been lucky enough to see a few of these in operation, but none more spectacular

Interior of the Vigili del Fuoco station, complete with an AW139, at Milan Malpensa.

The impressive training rig at Manchester airport in full flow.

or impressively designed than the one at Manchester Airport. The £2.6 million, 26-tonne 747/767/ MD11 dual-fuelled airport rescue and fire-fighting training simulator can be utilised to present many different scenarios, both internally and externally. These can be selected individually or in combination and include engine, undercarriage, wing and fuselage fires as well as running fuel fires using LPG or, more realistically, aviation kerosene.

   This training certainly has the feel of the real thing, even standing some distance away from the rig, the heat produced is substantial. When much closer and inside the fire truck, I detected no

Spraying the training rig at Milan Malpensa.

Foam being used on the training rig.

Fighting the fire from inside the Oshkosh Striker.

Left: Using hand lines to fight an engine fire.

Below left: It can get scary when you come this close to a fire.

Below right: Flash over.

Geneva Airport's 737 cabin trainer.

noticeable change in temperature despite the nearness of an impressive and dangerous-looking fire. This was much different to previous visits to training facilities when firefighters were still using hoses, which they call 'hand lines', with me a short distance behind, photographing the action. Furthermore, the 'inside' scenarios are quite frightening, particularly the scenarios that recreate a 'flash over' where fire runs at speed over the ceiling. After each scenario, the tenders are refilled in readiness not only for the next exercise but in case of a real callout during the training.

Many airports will have old aircraft, in full or in part, that serve as training aids for the evacuation or searching of aircraft cabins. These can often be rare aircraft, such as the Boeing 737-200 at Geneva. Formerly F-GCJL, it is one of the oldest remaining 737s in Europe, if not the world. It was the 71st 737 to be built and was delivered in September 1968 to United Airlines as N9029U.

Fire-fighters rotate through various RFFS roles, including a spell in the watch tower overlooking the airfield. Should there be an incident, this fire-fighter, as well as potentially initiating the call out, would also contact various people and organisations including the region's external fire service, police, ambulance and senior airport RFFS staff, possibly even rail authorities, if power to overhead cables feeding the airport railway station need to be temporarily cut.

Although none of us actually want it to happen, just what would happen in the event of a real aircraft emergency? Time is of the essence, and with this in mind every opportunity is taken to shave off time here and there. For example, when the alarm is sounded from ATC, this can automatically open the doors to the vehicle bays in the fire-fighting hub. When vehicles are started, the power supplies connected at the rear can be automatically ejected, saving about 30 seconds. This might not seem a lot, but this is just over 15 per cent of the maximum time allowed for the RFFS to reach the site in need. Plus would you like to be in a fire for 10 seconds longer, never mind 30! Emergencies are classified by type and although very much

Faro watch tower, overlooking the airfield.

the majority, not all of them are aircraft related. By far one of the largest number of incidents are classed as 'Local Standby'. This is where an inbound aircraft is known, or is suspected to have developed a defect that would not normally get in the way of a safe landing, for instance, a cockpit indication that the aircraft landing gear is not fully locked into position for landing. 'Aircraft Ground Incidents' are just what they sound like; it is when an aircraft on the ground has an emergency situation other than an accident that requires the attendance of the emergency services. Allied to this are such things as hazardous materials that may be involved, including spillages, which are not necessarily the obvious fuel ones. Some of the more unpleasant clear-up operations have included spillage of bull semen, and on another occasion the contents of an aircraft's toilet tank. An 'Aircraft Full Emergency' is when an aircraft in the air is, or is suspected to be, in such difficulties that there is a danger of an accident. Notification of this is most often initiated by the captain of the aircraft. Should ATC believe an accident is inevitable, then it can be classified as an 'Aircraft Accident Imminent'.

Left: **The power supply connected at the rear of the fire-fighting vehicle can be automatically ejected to save time.**

Below: **Fire vehicles attending a minor incident.**

A 737 transponder set to 7700.

The captain of a flight is in command of what happens unless circumstances take it out of his or her control. For instance, I was once told by an airport fire chief that for some incidents, such as an undercarriage fire, it is actually better to keep passengers on board. This is because the fire service will be able to deal with such an incident quickly and effectively with no danger to life. Whereas, if the decision is made to evacuate an aircraft, there is almost certainly going to be some level of injury in the process of evacuation, either from people clamouring to get off or due to hitting the ground awkwardly when using the evacuation slide. If circumstances are not rapidly progressing, discussions will be had between the fire chief and the captain as to the best course of action.

Other types of aircraft emergencies include bomb threats, either in the air and on the ground, or when an aircraft at, or inbound to an airport, is known or thought to have been hijacked. These

An airport safety vehicle at Townsville, Australia.

Fire-fighters cutting the roof off a vehicle.

situations may be indicated by a 'squawk code' (officially known as a transponder code) being transmitted by the aircraft's transponder, which is used by ATC radar to identify a specific aircraft. There are three emergency codes: 7500 indicates that the aircraft has been hijacked; 7600 means the aircraft has lost communication with ATC, which may even result in the aircraft being cleared to land using light signals; and 7700 is used to communicate that there is some form of emergency on board and that the aircraft will be flown by the crew in response to the emergency rather than first requesting instructions from ATC. This is relative to the code of aviators, which is to first aviate then navigate and finally communicate.

Even though airports have a strict speed limits, often around 20mph, with safety officers to police these, vehicle accidents attended and rehearsed by emergency services, though it is possible that airport crew may attend nearby incidents off airport grounds as well. In fact, I was told of an incident where airport fire crews attended when a famous footballer crashed his new Aston Martin in the tunnel system under the airports runways. In addition, the skills learnt and practised can also apply to aircraft incidents.

Thankfully, life isn't all about training for aviation emergencies. On the island of Barra (incidentally the only airport in the world using a beach for scheduled airline services) airport fire crews are called out far more frequently to help stranded dolphins or seals in the nearby bay than for any reason connected with the aircraft operations.

Chapter 5
Pushing Tin and ATC

Hollywood's attempts at aviation movies generally range from the ridiculous to the staggeringly horrendous, perhaps a DC9 taking off and changing mid-flight into a 737 then landing after flying the Atlantic in a couple of hours, or a complete removal of safety procedures in films involving ATC. *Pushing Tin*, made back in 1999 was at least supposed to be a comedy, and this made it just about watchable.[1] However, the 2018 film *2:22* was, at best, the worst ever aviation-themed film and probably did inordinate amounts of damage to anybody with a nervous disposition towards flying. If you tried to watch this film with any level of common sense, let alone aviation knowledge, you probably turned it off at the phrase 'Punch it!' and are still laughing uncontrollably many months later. Fortunately, the real world of ATC is

Brussels Airlines' Red Devil A320 beneath the Air Traffic Control (ATC) tower at Brussels National Airport.

---

1 'Pushing tin' is a slang term used by ATC. It references the direction of aircraft by ATC through the skies and onto the ground in an efficient and orderly fashion. It was made popular by the 1999 film of the same name.

nothing like what Hollywood would have us believe. Behind the glass, the visual control rooms at the top of the world's airports ATC towers contain a quiet and calm group of men and women moving aircraft around the skies and airport ramp.

You might think that, with all the space there is in the air, aircraft could simply fly from A to B in a straight line. Unfortunately, that would be chaotic with current capabilities, so air traffic is actually concentrated into areas and routes to help control and keep aircraft safely apart. Area controllers manage a portion of this total airspace, taking flights from, or passing them to, the controllers at the airport. At smaller airports or in more remote areas, controllers at airports may look after aircraft at greater distance. Yet, did you know that some airports do not have controllers at the airport at all? London City Airport has become the first major international airport in the world to be fully controlled by a remote digital ATC tower. The tower controllers are actually situated 115km away at National Air Traffic Services (NATS) main ATC centre in Swanwick, Hampshire. Instead of looking out of real windows, an 'enhanced reality' view is used via a state-of-the-art 50m digital control 'tower', which is, in simple terms, a huge bank of screens fed by 16 high-definition cameras and sensors mounted on a mast to capture a 360-degree view of the airfield, then relayed through a super-fast fibre connection to a room at Swanwick. A dedicated team of controllers use the live footage, an audio feed from the airfield and radar information to instruct aircraft movements in and out of the airport. They can even use the cameras to zoom in on anything should they need to.

But regardless of where they do it, just how do they do what they do? How do you 'push tin'? The size of an airport's operation very much determines the number of staff in the control tower. I visited the Greek island of Skiathos back in 2014, and even in the busy summer period there was just a single controller performing all the tasks. Skiathos does, however, have one interesting and non-standard

Each controller has an array of screens providing different types of information.

Above: At Skiathos, there is just a single controller performing all the tasks.

Right: Traffic lights stop cars from passing under the approach when an aircraft is landing.

procedure with each movement as traffic lights need switching on to stop traffic on the road that runs round the 02 threshold. This is due to arriving aircraft passing very low over the road. Although no longer in use, this system was in operation many decades ago at Manchester Airport, when the nearby main road passed through the airfield over the runway. At major international airports, tasks will be split across a number of people situated in the tower, or VCR, right at the top behind the massive tinted windows overlooking the airport.

Exactly how each VCR is set up will vary from airport to airport. In general, there will be controllers responsible for aircraft movement on the ground and providing slot times and the relevant clearances to departing aircraft. There are separate controllers for each runway, whether for

Above: A controller looking over the ramp at Manchester Airport.

Left: Control tower at Singapore Changi Airport

arrival or departure. Overseeing the VCR is a watch manager. All controllers rotate through all the positions in the VCR, changing after a 30-minute break following a period of approximately 60–90 minutes of plugged-in controlling, which not only maintains currency in each position but keeps staff fresh throughout the day.

As well as maintaining direct communications with the aircrew, ATC officers co-ordinate with each other and other ATC units via telephone, regarding various operational matters.

Aircraft inbound to major airports usually follow a specific route known as a Standard Arrival Route (STAR), sometimes to a prescribed

ATC station at Manchester Airport.

holding stack.[2] When there is room in the inbound sequence, aircraft are directed (through a system called radar vectoring) from approximately 10,000ft and 40 nautical miles out and given heading, height and speed instructions to arrange a loose order of arrival. Aircraft are then passed to the next contact, who has the responsibility of putting this loose arrangement into an exact order for landing. Generally, there is an attempt to keep aircraft three miles apart in the latter stages of the approach but the controllers will also take into account any requirements for extra spacing due to turbulence, wake vortex[3] or departures, whether using an Instrument Landing System (ILS) or landing visually.

Inside the VCR, the overriding impression is of cool calmness. If you ignore the magnificent view of the airfield out of the panoramic windows, you could almost think this was any other office workplace until, of course, you look at what is on the computer screens at each workstation. Modern ATC systems differ from the past, as what is seen on the controllers' screens today is no longer the actual radar return but a computer-generated view based on those radar returns. In fact, it is a much more complex version of the flight tracking apps widely available now, with a great deal of information that grants a good deal of manipulation and flexibility to assist controllers in their work. The true radar screens are situated in the engineering department.

---

2 A holding stack is when aircraft go around and around in a racetrack pattern, over a radio navigation point, 1,000ft apart vertically. This is to control arrivals into an airport. Aircraft will, in turn, be taken from the bottom of this stack to be vectored into an airport, at which point each aircraft above will in turn be instructed to descend to the next level.

3 Aircraft may create spirals of wind called wake vortices, which can create difficulties for following aircraft. Winglets on aircraft reduce these vortices, which in turn reduce fuel burn.

Computer-generated radar screen and flight progress strips at the watch manager's station.

Everything is now digital, even down to the flight progress strips. These simple yet successful products were originally strips of paper on which information about each flight is printed and on which each controller handling that aircraft would write the specific instructions given to the crew.

A physical flight progress strip.

These strips were held on plastic carriers that were simply passed from one controller to another along with the responsibility for that flight. Not that different to the old token system used in the early days of train travel, which ensured only one train was on a specific track at any one time.

Flight progress strips are still used to keep tabs on what the aircraft should be doing and with whom, but they are now an editable image on a screen, sent electronically from one controller to another. As with

Flight progress strips in use at Skiathos.

the originals these electronic strips contain information such as call sign, flight number, departure and destination airports, aircraft type, estimated time of arrival (ETA), estimated time of departure (ETC) and the Standard Instrument Departure or STAR.

Although the equipment mentioned so far is of the utmost importance, it is by no means the only items at the disposal of controllers at an airport. Each station can include items such as an Aerodrome Traffic Monitor (ATM) to monitor aircraft in the air approaching/departing and flying in the vicinity of the airport. A Surface Movement radar (particularly useful in low visibility conditions when it is near-impossible to see surface movements with the naked eye) monitors aircraft and vehicles on the ground, including runways, a meteorological station provides up-to-the-minute weather reports and an aerodrome lighting panel allows for the control of ground-level lighting. All of this technology, however, requires one, very important, sensor, according to one controller: the original 'Mark 1 eyeball'.

Despite the levels of pressure that can be on a controller's shoulders, I can assure you whenever I visited an ATC facility everything was calm and organised, aircraft were directed smoothly into and out of the world's airports and definitely nobody said 'Punch it'.[4]

---

4   While used in a multitude of aviation movies, this quote was arguably made most famous by Han Solo while flying the Millennium Falcon in *Star Wars: Episode V – The Empire Strikes Back.*

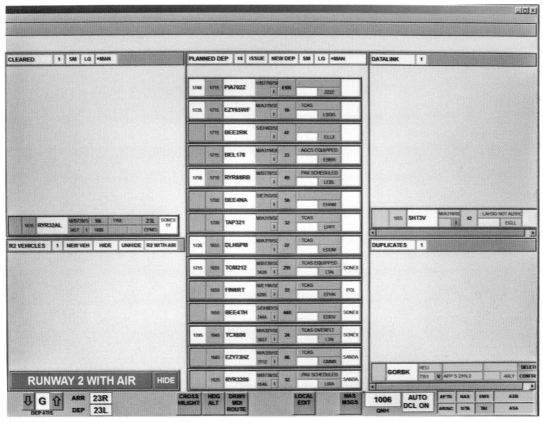

Digital flight progress strips in use at Manchester.

Even with all this information on tap, you cannot do without the 'Mark 1 eyeball'.

Chapter 6

Freight Operations: From Fish to Ferraris

These days, aircraft are pretty much a tube of aluminium or carbon fibre, and us passengers sit in about the top two thirds, give or take. Below us are our bags full of suntan lotion and swimwear. However, luggage is not the only thing that travels underneath us as we fly.

Before the COVID-19 pandemic, around 50 per cent of all the world's airfreight actually flew in the hold of commercial passenger services. This is why there were some difficulties in the supply chain during the height of the pandemic, as, all of a sudden, this capacity to transport goods simply no longer

existed. The use of full freight aircraft and passenger aircraft converted to carry lightweight freight on the main deck in addition to the hold did fill some of this lost capacity, but it simply couldn't do it all, nor could it match the route structure.

AKE containers being loaded into the hold of an Emirates A380.

KLM 747-400 COMBIs at Amsterdam Schiphol.

The containers used for airfreight are collectively called Unit Load Devices (ULD). The most common size, designed to maximise the available space by fitting into the curved space on the bottom of the fuselage of modern aircraft types, is called an AKE[5], otherwise known as an LD3. There are also some aircraft called COMBIs, which have the main deck split to take passengers in one section and freight in another, and on these aircraft the types of cargo can be very diverse. Cargo and baggage in or on ULDs are loaded using scissor lift devices designed specifically for that purpose. In smaller aircraft types, both passenger bags and any freight will be loaded piece by piece. In fact, sometimes items are loaded in this way in larger aircraft too, depending on the facilities available and the airline's processes. This is when the elevated conveyor belt devices are used, with one person at the bottom feeding it bags with another person in the hold stacking the bags inside.

How, though, does this freight get to the aircraft in the first place? General cargo is delivered to the airline or freight forwarder's warehouse where it goes through processing, which includes shipment specific and security checks. If the product is perishable or deemed to be dangerous or if they are pharmaceutical, then they will be stored in product-specific dedicated areas. Higher level checks on these products will then happen, as well as checks on labelling and a determination of whether the product is even safe to travel on the route or aircraft type. It will also be scanned or

---

5   The letters used for different containers signify different things. The first letter indicates the type of air container, for example the 'A' is for 'Certified Aircraft Container'. The second letter refers to the dimensions of the base of the container, for example, 'K' means that the measurements of the container are 1.534x1.562m². The third character indicates one of two different things, depending on whether it is a container or a pallet. When it is a container, it determines its shape, contour and load capacity. When it is a pallet, it refers to the type of network, mesh or execution system used.

Above: Bags being loaded onto an easyJet A321.

Right: An Air Bridge Cargo Pharma 747 freighter rotating with another cargo of pharmaceuticals.

X-rayed. Pharmaceutical products also need to be kept refrigerated. The very cold storage temperatures required by some of the COVID-19 vaccines initially created a number of issues, not only with reaching and maintaining the temperature but also the sheer amount of storage required with very little warning.

The various shipments arriving by road and aircraft will be combined together in one or more of the ULDs that are destined for each departing flight. Some may have priority over others if space is at a premium. Some dangerous goods are not allowed to be packed along with certain other products or even in the near vicinity, so this must also be taken into account. Once the flight is ready to accept the cargo, the ULDs will be loaded onto dollies, taking into account the configuration of each aircraft type. It is vitally important that weight is distributed in the correct manner on an aircraft, as the centre of gravity has to be correct to ensure the aircraft will actually get and stay airborne. These are then towed airside, and on arrival at the aircraft they are moved from the dolly directly onto the aircraft. Pharmaceutical ULDs will be the last to move, needing some form of active refrigeration for as long as

A DHL A300F being loaded with ULDs full of freight.

Above: A Prime Air 737-800SF.

Left: Unit Load Devices (ULD) being loaded from the warehouse onto dollies.

possible due to the highly perishable nature of the product. The captain will have been made aware of any dangerous or specific cargo on board in what is called the load sheet, which details the total weight of the aircraft including its passengers, from which the flight crew can work out various parameters for the flight including how much fuel to take in board.

ULD being loaded onto a UPS 767 freighter.

A very large percentage of cargo travels by night.

The Antonov AN225 Mriya. It was the world's largest aircraft until it's destruction during the conflict in Ukraine.

DHL ramp at East Midlands Airport.

While 50 per cent of air freight is sent in the belly of passenger aircraft, the remaining 50 per cent is transported on dedicated freight aircraft. These aircraft are, in essence, huge empty tubes waiting to be filled with anything from your most recent Amazon order through to an F1 car. Some aircraft are freight versions of passenger aircraft, some have been converted from passenger operations, and some have been designed specifically with freight in mind and can be very large indeed. Up to the sad events in the Ukraine, the largest of these was the Antonov AN 225, a one-of-a-kind aircraft initially designed to carry the Soviet 'Buran' space shuttle.

Because of the nature of some shipments and the requirement to park in proximity to the freight forwarder's warehouse, cargo aircraft are required to park in specific areas of the airport, often away from the main terminal buildings. If you happen to taxi out in the right direction at an airport that handles plenty of airfreight, you might catch sight of an innocuous-looking device that forms part of Project *CYCLAMEN*. This programme was initiated to manage the risk of non-conventional terrorism in the UK following Al-Qaeda's attacks against the US in 2001. These devices have the capability to detect radiological and nuclear materials. Any shipments from outside the UK must be driven though these portals, which trigger an alarm to Border Force staff should anything be detected. In practice, these devices do not create any real delays as the freight simply requires driving through.

It is fairly common to transport cars by air. Delivery and acceptance into the airline or freight forwarders's warehouse is more-or-less the same as for any other product. However, the process of getting it into the aircraft may not be. The majority of cars can fit onto one pallet. Some are too big to fit on one pallet. If this is the case, they must be loaded onto two, with half the weight of the car being carried by each pallet. When pallets are loaded, they are pushed along tracks on the floor of the hold and then locked into position. Manoeuvring two pallets at one time, through a door, around a corner and into the aircraft, with an expensive car on top, is a challenge. A team of highly trained personnel are employed to ensure the car is loaded correctly into the aircraft, it is then strapped down to secure it for the flight. There are even cases where the car has to be driven tiny amounts to get it to fit.

Freight is very important to an airline as well as the regions it serves. It has been estimated that 15–20 tonnes of air cargo is worth the equivalent of 30–40 economy passenger seats, when both are on passenger planes. Such is the significance freight and cargo that airlines have even painted aircraft in special designs, from Alaska Airlines' 'Salmon Thirty Salmon' liveries, which highlights the importance of salmon exports for Alaska, and Martinair's flower design on one of its MD11Fs, which signified the importance of flower exports from the Netherlands.

These devices have the capability to detect radiological and nuclear materials.

Cars are regular travellers on cargo flights.

Alaska Airlines' 'Salmon Thirty Salmon'-liveried 737-800.

A Martinair MD-11F with a flower design.

Chapter 7

Riches, Royalty and Rescue

There are many places around an airport complex that, although not staff areas, are unlikely to be seen by the vast majority of general travellers. These are the areas with differing levels of private facilities on offer to those who wish to pay, or for those whose security dictates a need to be kept separate. Nowadays there are lounges that are available at a more accessible cost, but this has not always been the case.

Airport lounges have historically been the domain of those who get to 'turn left' on entering an aircraft, enjoying either business or first class seats. Generally speaking, the food and beverages on offer in these facilities are of a substantially better quality than is on offer to the masses. Spa treatments are the norm, signature cocktails are in abundance and relaxation or business suites are available depending on your needs. Airlines may have their own Business Class lounge (or sometimes multiple, as is the case with British Airways at London Heathrow, Delta at Atlanta, or Korean Air at Seoul, to name just a few) at their home base, given the larger numbers of Business Class travellers passing through the many flights that airline will be operating there. If an airline has a large presence at a particular airport, it may have its own business lounge if it is cost effective to do so. For instance, British Airways operates its own, albeit quite small, facility at New York's JFK airport.

Rendezvous Executive Lounge at the Isle of Man airport of Ronaldsway.

Dining area in Qatar Airways First Class lounge at Doha.

Skyteam lounge at Heathrow Terminal 4.

In some cases, an airline that is part of one of the big airline alliances, such as One World, Star Alliance and Skyteam, may use the home lounge of another alliance member. If not, then they may have one of their own for the passengers of the group's airlines. However, the further an airline is from its own facility, the further its passengers are from the brand and service the airline promotes. For instance, on a trip from Bangkok to Manchester via Frankfurt, I had the opportunity to have a free Thai head and neck massage and authentic Thai food, however this is not something that is necessarily available to Thai Airways' passengers in other parts of the world. Thai Airways are not exclusive in offering treatments and specialties, for instance Cathay passengers at Hong Kong International also get a massage, this time, however, it's feet! Or, for those with an eye for history, American Airlines lounge at JFK has a speakeasy-esque bar. A number of lounges also have private external viewing areas, providing a breath of fresh air while you look out over the airport, and, in the case of Swiss International's First Class lounge at Zurich, that view extends to the Alps.

Speaking of First class lounges, at a basic level, they are not that different from airline-specific business class lounges. They do, of course, have some noticeable differences and can even be completely separate buildings from the rest of the terminal complex. Lufthansa at Frankfurt and Singapore Airlines at its home base of Changi, Singapore, are just two that have implemented separate buildings. The food will be gourmet standard and there will be treatments and airline specialties on offer. The service is akin to the best five-star hotels the world has to offer, from restaurant staff to the customer service team.

However, one of the main privileges awarded to first class customers is space – enormous amounts of space. This space gives passengers the opportunity to be in quiet, uninterrupted areas to work, relax and, if you wish to hide away, there are personal bedrooms on offer, as well as movie theatres and play

Singapore Airlines' First Class terminal at Changi.

rooms for kids. This space, combined with a high level of decor gives a feeling of opulence that guests expect. Some airlines take this opulence a stage further, with the lounge housing historic works of local art or items of national significance. The Qatar Airways First Class lounge at Doha is a perfect example of this, with square metres of space seemingly given over to nothing in particular. Then you come across an Islamic fine art installation or artefacts on loan from Doha's Museum of Islamic Art.

First class lounges may offer special access to the aircraft, keeping its passengers away from the general throng. The best example of this was where Concorde passengers would board the aircraft directly from the Concorde Lounge at London Heathrow. This lounge was up a level again from the 'standard' First Class lounge. Originally created exclusively for passengers on the Concorde services, it is still in existence to this day. There is even a new breed of lounges available to anybody with the requisite amount of funds that means you can be picked up from home, transported to the lounge, fed and watered in luxury whilst waiting until the last minute, to be transported by a limo across the airport ramp to your commercial flight.

If your need for privacy cannot be satiated by flying First Class on a commercial airline, even with all the benefits this affords, then you will need to utilise a private jet facility run by a Fixed Base Operator (FBO). While these facilities are not necessarily as opulent, what they do offer is speed. With their own security and ultra-short distance to the aircraft, passengers can turn up and take off minutes later, away from prying eyes. On a visit to Reykjavik Airport, I was shown the FBO, which is a small and unassuming facility much loved by many a celebrity as it is a quick, easy and very private way into the country, which is situated pretty midway between the US and Europe. So much so that Tom Cruise, apparently a regular visitor, had left a note of thanks. As well as privacy from the public eye, there may be other reasons to choose a more private terminal. At one FBO, I spotted a section of the pending

Qatar Airways' Al Safwa First Class Lounge at Doha.

Skylink Services' Executive Terminal at Larnaca, Cyprus.

Milan Linate's Prime Executive Terminal.

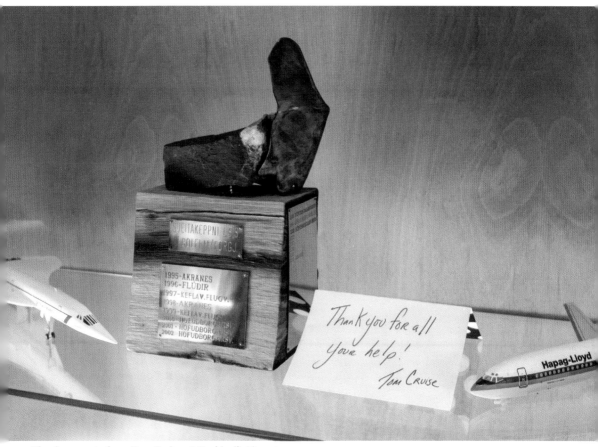

Thank you note from Tom Cruise at Reykjavik Airport.

flights board which had a firearms certificate on it with a casual post-it note stuck to it stating that the company were awaiting an email stating just what guns were being brought in.

What if the requirement to be far away from the crowd is more of a need than a desire? Then you would find yourself in an airport's secure VIP facility, designed to accommodate heads of state and governmental visits. Almost always situated remote from the main airport buildings, these facilities are often co-located within the military or governmental side to an airport, should it have one. These areas are most often on the far side of the airports runway system, and you may well get a tap on the shoulder if you point your camera that way. I have been on official visits to many an airport, escorted by airport management, only to be told to take care when photographing the commercial operations in case I should catch a military aircraft way in the background. When flying in and out of Busan in South Korea, an announcement is made on board prior to taxiing and landing, warning of pretty dire consequences if you do not take heed of the 'no photography through the aircraft windows' order!

The VIP facilities at Naples Italy are a good example of this. The facilities are not necessarily glamorous, more pleasantly functional, as its guests are only staying for a minimum amount of time on their way to and from official engagements (or a luxury holiday). There was an instance where I met with the CEO of the airport who knew the Major in charge of the airport's military facilities very well. I was taken through to the VIP room to be shown what is, in essence, the visitors book, its pages open at the entry for the then-Duchess of Cornwall's visit on 1 April 2017. Speaking of the UK royal family, London Heathrow airport has such a facility for the UK's royal family, called the Windsor Suite.

Aeronautica Militare at Naples Airport.

Camilla Shand
Duchessa di Cornovaglia e Rothesay
Principessa di Galles

Napoli, 1° Aprile 2017

Signature of Camilla, the then-Duchess of Cornwall, in the official visitors book at Naples.

These facilities are ultra-secure, and the ramp outside may house not only that country's government and royal fleets but also military transports, and even security and emergency service fleets, which can mean a diverse range of aircraft on display. In Ibiza, there is a SAMU Bell 412EP air ambulance and, at Naples, the Italian Coast Guard and the 6th Flight Department of the state police are represented at the

A SAMU Bell 412EP Air Ambulance at Ibiza.

An Italian Coast Guard AW139 at Naples.

airport. Muscat Airport in Oman houses Embraer 170s of the local security forces and A320s of the Air Force transport division, as well as the Sultan's private 747. Brussels has a base with military and VIP transport A321s, ERJ135LRs and C130s. To a lesser degree, Larnaca has police helicopters sharing the ramp outside its FBO.

Oman security services' E170.

An Oman Air Force A320.

A Belgian Air Force A321.

A Belgian Air Force ERJ 135LR.

A Belgian Air Force C130.

A Cyprus Police Aviation Unit Agusta Bell 412EP.

In Australia, these facilities house the aircraft of the famous Royal Flying Doctor Service in addition to the various states' rescue helicopters. Back in August 2015, I had the pleasure of joining Queensland Government Air Rescue for a day. However, and in true Aussie style, after joining them on a patient transfer, they dropped me off in the bush, purportedly just for a quick photo, but they left me there for around 15 minutes before screaming past at a large rate of knots.

RFDS' Beechcraft B200 Super King Air.

A QGAir Bell 412HP landing in the Australian bush.

Flypast of a QGAir Bell 412HP.

Planning for the mission in the QGAir Rescue Operations room.

Chapter 8

Securing You, the Country Borders and the Environment

There are many different types of security at an airport, some of which are very much in our faces including patrolling armed police and, in some cases, a country's armed forces. There are also the men and women at what passengers would term 'security', the people operating the scanning machines and wiping a tiny cloth over our bags. Then there are the more covert or less visual levels of security. A passenger would most likely first come into contact with what might be termed local security. the people who ensure we don't park in the wrong place or inadvertently walk though an entrance not designed for passenger use. Another very visible level of security you might come across is the local, almost certainly armed, police. The role of the local police varies tremendously from country to country, but in general terms they are tasked with the safety of that country's airports. Often, airport police are cross-trained to have other skills that might be required, such as emergency first aid. Sometimes, the officers are part of the country's main police or armed forces. Other countries have set up separate units, some of which even have customs' duties. For example, in the UK, following a terrorist alert at Heathrow in 1974, the army was deployed to the incident due to local police being unarmed, and as a result airports now have dedicated forces with a large proportion of officers being armed. Project Servator is a policing tactic utilised at airports. It aims to disrupt a range of criminal activity, including terrorism, while providing a reassuring presence for the public. It is used by a number of UK police forces and New South Wales Police Force in Australia.

What is often termed 'going through security' be a passenger's most dreaded part of any trip. This process has changed considerably over the years, owing to terrorist atrocities such as Lockerbie and 9/11. Unfortunately, we now live in a world where aviation is a massive target for those wishing to promote whatever cause they feel is just, often in the most horrific and ultimately headline-grabbing of ways. This is why the security journey has become increasingly complicated over the years. When I first started to be involved in aviation many decades ago, I would arrive at my local airport, go to an internal phone, ring up a contact and within a few minutes I would be through an internal door and out onto the apron. Nowadays, at a minimum, that would likely be a firing offence for the employee and possibly an arrestable one!

Security staff are looking for items that might cause damage to either the aircraft or people onboard. With the many different ways terrorists have found to get contraband onboard, the security fraternity must keep up with an ever-increasing list of types of products to detect either by machine, personal search or by using trained-for-purpose dog. The previous bias towards X-rays and metal detectors is changing, with a move towards CT scanners. These scanners see in 3D, which is not only a better view but is something that will reduce wait times as passengers will no longer need to remove electronics from bags or put liquids aside in a little bag. Older X-ray systems provided a single view of the tray's contents, generally from underneath, requiring items to be spread out to

A metal detector and single-view X-ray machine.

CT scanning technology, such as these at Milan Linate, is now making its way into airport security.

prevent confusion, even to an experienced operator. More recent X-ray machines added in a sideways view and colour to help the operator piece together what they are looking at. However, CT scanners will be game-changing, as they enable the operator to manipulate the image digitally and pull it completely apart, looking at individual items or making them invisible to see items underneath. This does come at a cost, however. Single-view X-ray machines cost around £20,000–30,000, with dual-view at around £50,000–60,000. The CT scanners, however, may cost anything between £250,000 and £750,000, so it's a massive investment. The same cost differential is notable when comparing old-fashioned metal detectors with body scanners, where its around £20,000 vs £150,000, respectively. Newer security areas utilise a much larger which is required to optimise the benefits of using the new CT scanners. It allows for a speedier throughput, as, in shorter lanes, if a number of trays are rejected, then the whole lane can come to a grinding halt. Once rejected, these bags are likely to be swabbed using a trace detection system. At around £50,000, these small devices have an awful lot going in on inside. One way to think of it is imagine you handle some explosives, then you handle a bag and then someone else handles that bag before picking up their own, these kits can detect the explosive residue on the last bag. It is likely that the larger airports will transition to CT quickly, as you need the passenger numbers to justify the investment.

Have you ever wondered why you seem to always be singled out for the wipe down of your carryon luggage when there is actually nothing untoward in it? Well, you might just have bad luck, but it is probably because of the types of items you have in the bag. I know this because I am one of those people. For obvious reasons, I always carry my photographic equipment with me at all times and never put into the hold. As you can see on an airport's displayed list of prohibited items, there are not only items that are designed to do harm but also those that might inadvertently do so. Items

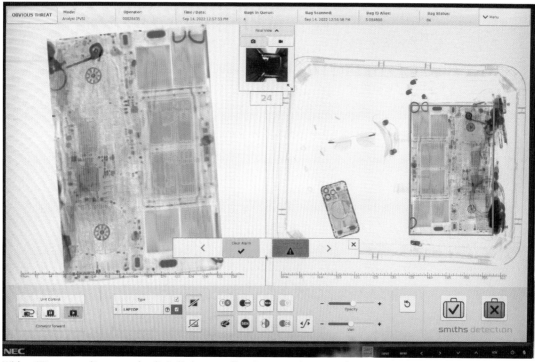

With a CT scanner, items can be digitally 'removed' and screened separately.

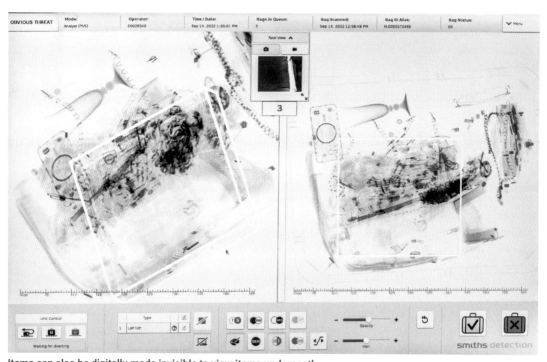

Items can also be digitally made invisible to view items underneath.

Longer lanes are required to make full use of the throughput of a CT scanner.

that are knowingly being attempted to smuggle through security are often hidden inside other, more benign items. As some airports do not require camera equipment to be removed from a bag, I was more than happy not to have to empty it out, although this did eventually lead to a bit of a situation. It was only after a series of trips with my bag being swabbed on every occasion that, having quite a chatty security person, I asked why this might be the case. I was told that my camera equipment is quite dense in nature and to be sure nothing might be lurking inside, it was pulled aside to be checked over. Normally that is just a slight inconvenience, I am all for good security and always arrive at the airport in good time. However, on one occasion, I ended up with quite a lot of rather nervous and funny looks from my fellow passengers as on one trip out of Bremen in Germany, my bag was again in need of extra attention. However, this time, rather than the swab being taken at the end of the security station like at most airports, a rather large policeman arrived and marched me over to a room with the word 'Polizei' (Police) on the door to do the check. I have to say, I was a little perturbed by this myself.

Because many security officers will never see an actual threat in their whole career, to keep them sharp and motivated, there is something called threat image projection (TIP) on scanning machines, which randomly superimpose images of real threats onto passenger's bags to keep these officers on their toes. Even without these additions, you wouldn't believe what can actually end up in scanners. There are numerous reports of children climbing into baggage systems and then going through the X-ray and even, believe it or not, parents placing the baby carrier through… without removing the baby first. It has even been known for people to sleep in the machines. This is why the startup procedure requires a reversal of the belt first to ensure the tunnel is clear before X-rays are turned on.

Don't worry though, as the machines used in public areas are about 50 times less powerful than those found in a medical X-ray, so it's unlikely to be harmful.

It is not just passengers who go through a security procedure when going airside. Employees also have to take off shoes, belts and coats and send them though the X-ray machine. All vehicles, including emergency services, unless on a blue light call, entering Airside areas have to be checked. Whilst the occupants go through the 'normal' passenger experience, the vehicle is checked thoroughly inside and out (and underneath) for anything deemed a risk. Contractors' equipment will need X-raying and possibly even be pre-cleared. There has been many a time I have had to pre-clear my photographic equipment, although this pre-clearance never seems to make it to the people on the ground. Any contractors or visitors of any sort to airside areas will need to be security checked in advance, later collecting a pass from the airport pass office or department, depending on the protocols.

The tone of the security checks changes somewhat once arriving at a destination. At the point of arrival, the focus is more about not letting items, or indeed people, into the country. Items countries don't allow in can vary tremendously and who polices this will vary also, although it is generally some type of border force. In the UK, Border Force is a law enforcement command within the Home Office. It facilitates the legitimate movement of individuals and goods, whilst preventing those that would cause harm from entering the UK via immigration and customs' checks. Be aware that you are being watched whilst collecting your bags from the baggage carousel, and depending on your body language you may well be chosen for a search before you even decide which channel to take. The role is not just to find prohibited goods, be they illicit or just too many cigarettes, they are also there to work with other security services to ensure foreign nationals are visiting the country for valid reasons and have the correct documentation. If they cannot do anything about their suspicions there and then, they would alert the police and, security services to people of interest.

Obviously, guns, knives, chemical and electromagnetic weapons, plastic explosives and nuclear materials are on every country's prohibited lists alongside some, at first glance, quite amusing items. Different countries have different priorities about what is being searched for, with some being rather odd. Australia is very hot on protecting the biodiversity of the country and has a long list of foodstuffs (including fruits and pulses – anything in which a creature, no matter how small, could hide) that are not allowed into and out of the country. It also does not allow the importation of dog collars, novelty erasers, fly swatters and 'ice pipes', whatever they are! Harry Potter-licensed products fall foul of the Iranian authorities, as do Barbie dolls and the novel *The Da Vinci Code*. Canada has banned baby walkers, whilst in Japan you can be deported for having Vicks inhaler and in Singapore there is a $1000 fine for having chewing gum. Possibly most strange of all, it is illegal to take mineral water into Nigeria!

Behind the scenes, there is plenty more going on. In an airport mail centre, there are more screening machines as well as dogs trained to find anything from illicit drugs to money and explosives. Dogs are also often out and about in the terminal and security areas constantly checking you and your luggage. Israel has also started to instigate the use of mice for explosives' detection, as they are apparently easy to train, have an excellent sense of smell and are easy to transport. On the subject of different animals, researchers in Germany have also supposedly found out that honeybees can be trained to detect drugs.

Your bags will also be screened on their way to the aircraft, the boundary of the airport will be patrolled, and the cabins of the aircraft you will be flying could also be searched. There are specialist machines to screen pallets of cargo for nuclear and radiological materials, as mentioned earlier.

There may also be specialist security for certain airlines and countries, if a greater threat is perceived. For instance, in Israel, all vehicles entering Ben Gurion Airport go through a preliminary security check before entering the airport perimeter. Armed officers search all vehicles whilst doing an initial screen of the occupants. Should anyone act nervously or suspiciously in their eyes, they will be sent for further screening. Regardless, all passengers will be questioned at the check-in desk. Following this, you will be given a colour code that indicates the level of security checks you will have to undertake going forward. Your baggage also will go through extra measures. Not only will it be screened in X-ray machines and CT scanners, it will be placed in a pressure chamber designed to detonate any explosive devices that are designed to activate in low pressure. The Israeli national airline, El Al, used to have a military escort to the end of the runway, and still often have extra security on the ramp when its aircraft is on stand. Since the turn of the millennium, most of its aircraft have been fitted with systems to detect and defend against a missile in the early stages of an attack, making it the only airline in the world to do so.

Air marshals are also on every flight. These undercover agents may be armed, as they are on some flights in the US and other parts of the world. Of a more covert nature, specialist police forces such as 'Special Branch' and the Serious Organised Crime Agency in the UK are also constantly looking for known undesirables.

Not every security force is looking for undesirables hell bent on destruction. At Thailand's airports, there are 'Tourist Police'. These officers are there to give assistance to hapless travellers should something go wrong, or they are just in need of a little signposting.

Tourist Assistance Centre, home of Bangkok Airport's Tourist Police.

Chapter 9

Help, Support and Guidance

When it comes to looking for help at an airport, the most obvious place to look is the information desk or look for customer services' staff walking the terminal areas. Customer services staff are very much front and centre of an airport terminal, and we will all, at some point in time, have availed ourselves of their services in some foreign or unfamiliar airport. Staff on the front line will often see the public at their most stressed, and stress can make people do odd things. The pandemic was scary for a lot of people. However, some Chinese nationals returning home from Italy at the height of the pandemic took very extreme precautions in a very strange direction. Terminal management at the airport showed me pictures of children completely covered with large plastic bags! Suffocation or Covid –clearly they were unsure which was worse! However, looking a little deeper, we find more specific assistance and sometimes from where we might not expect it!

An information desk at Singapore Changi.

Passengers with reduced mobility

Passengers with reduced mobility, known as PRMs, generally need a little bit of extra assistance when transiting through an airport. Heathrow reports that approximately 1.2 million PRMs travel through the airport annually. The International Civil Aviation Organization has defined a PRM as a person whose mobility is reduced by physical incapacity, both sensory and locomotor, or intellectual deficiencies due to advanced age, illness or other disability when using transport, and whose situation requires special attention. Wheelchair-bound passengers may require assistance through the various stages of their journey to the aircraft. If they do not have one of their own, or somebody to push it, then there is a need for the airport to assist them through the various stages of their journey to the aircraft.

Airports generally classify PRMs in one of three categories similar to the following, albeit sometimes using different vocabulary. The majority of airlines use a letter category:

R: The passenger may only need a wheelchair to cover longer distances; climbing stairs may be possible and will be self-sufficient in flight.
S: The passenger can walk short distances but cannot climb stairs, but is self-sufficient in flight.
C: The passenger always needs a wheelchair and requires assistance to board and during flight.

Passengers may require the use of a hi-lift vehicle called an Ambulift to get them on or off the aircraft. This is a vehicle based on the scissor lift principle.

Safety is at the heart of all Airside operations, and there are standard procedures to ensure that mobility aids are must used and transported in a way that is safe for both the user and the airline/airport. For instance, in an ideal world, there should be a second wheelchair Airside so that the barrier between landside and Airside is not breached. Furthermore, where passengers are using motorised

Above and overleaf: Ambulift vehicles provide access to wheelchair users.

devices, these have to be made safe in a prescribed manner prior to loading to avoid inadvertent operation in flight, resulting in short circuiting and fires.

Chaplaincies

What happens when the problem becomes a little complicated, or there is no linear progression or obvious route to resolution? This might come from a source you wouldn't expect. Airport prayer rooms, either multi-denominational or specific to a religion or faith, can generally be quite easy to find and are often signposted in the terminal area. However, over 170 airports also have what are known as chaplaincies, similar to those that were attached to military units, and, in fact, airport chaplaincies have been formed around the core principals of the military versions. Although part of a chaplain's role is to manage the prayer rooms, their overriding principle is quite simply to help, guide and support passengers and airport staff through whatever problem or concern they might have. Be it simply helping a person navigate the complexities of

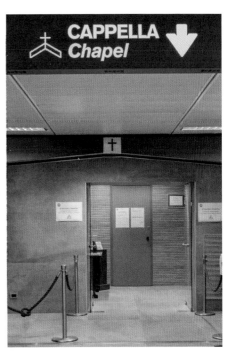

Right and below: The chapel at Milan Linate.

an airport journey through to assisting with some considerable life situations that involved travelling through an airport. The question of faith, or lack of it, is not necessarily of relevance here, as to avail yourself of a chaplain's help you do not necessarily need to believe, although spiritual guidance is on hand should it be required. These prayer rooms quite often attract people in need, as well as than those going to pray. For example, at an airport chapel in Italy, I found a lady who was simply in need of some peace after navigating a difficult personal situation. A chaplain's role is much more about empathising with the people that come into their orbit and helping them through to as satisfactory an outcome as possible.

One chaplain told me of a number of stories that demonstrate these principles quite well and also show that the real problem is not always the one that is front and centre. A Muslim student in his early 20s turned up at a major airport wanting to buy a ticket to see his girlfriend who lived in a different country. Not realising that nowadays you can't simply turn up at an airport, buy a ticket and get on board a plane, he was referred to the chaplaincy by customer services. This turned out to be rather more than just a quick visit, as this man had turned his back on his Muslim faith to become a Christian and as such had been ostracised by his family and was seeking a new life abroad. This story very aptly demonstrates a general theme that often runs through those in difficulty at an airport, that of leaving an old life and starting a new. More extreme versions of this theme can be seen when victims of exploitation or refugees arrive. The process of immigration can be quite scary. This is where the joint working with agencies like Border Force, the police and the Foreign Office comes into play to assist those who have been identified as 'at risk'.

Rough sleeping can also be a common sight in airports, and on my travels in something akin to the film 'The Terminal' I heard of one airport that had a very smart businessman who could often be seen on his laptop around the terminals, seemingly en route to some business meeting abroad. Not so, however, as due to a lineup of negative events he had found himself homeless and was, in effect, living at the airport. This person was eventually found accommodation by that airport's chaplain. At Rome Fiumicino, there is even a homeless centre on site that was linked with an onsite church.

Chaplaincies have come quite a way in their time and now have become part of airport emergency response teams, something that can be traced back to the 1985 Manchester Airport disaster.[6] However, as told to me by one chaplain, with his tongue firmly in his cheek, they spend the majority of their time 'wandering aimlessly around the terminals'. This might seem a little odd, but in fact this chaplain was actually quite proud of this and wore it somewhat of a badge of office, having heard the phrase spoken in a security training session describing the chaplaincy in that way. The way he saw it, he wanted staff and passengers to think that the chaplaincy has 'all the time in the world' for them, if they need support.

It's not just chaplaincies that do this type of work, other charitable organisations such as Travelcare at Heathrow and Travellors Aid at many US and Australian major airports do the same. Hopefully we will never need the type of assistance offered by these organisations, although it is heartening to know they exist if we do.

---

6 On 22 August 1985, 55 people died when a British Airtours Boeing 737-236 caught fire due to an uncontained engine failure whilst on take off from Manchester Airport. Toxic smoke from burning materials such as seats and fittings filled the cabin, resulting in the deaths of 53 passengers and two crew, the main cause of death being smoke inhalation. As a result of the accident, in what was described as 'a defining moment in the history of civil aviation', the Cranfield Institute did a large amount of research into the evacuation of aircraft in emergencies and combustible materials.

Chapter 10

All Creatures Great and Small

While I have mentioned birds when it comes to being a nuisance to aircraft and different animals' roles in security, there are many more animals in and around an airport. There are of course those that just find their way in: I have seen many different animals, from the very common rabbits and hares through to kangaroos at Cairns and, on the rough strips of Africa, it is not uncommon to have to do a flypast to scare away any number of different creatures before you can land.

Furthermore, when it comes to jobs for animals at airports, there are more than you might think. You may remember that grassed areas at airports are regularly mown to a certain length to discourage birds. However, vegetation is not always so easy to keep under control. Where it grows too is thick and deep, and cutting machinery is not an option, and/or worker safety may be an issue, some airports have

A hare running through the approach lights at Faro.

A Kangaroo trespasser at Cairns Airport, Australia.

employed animals to simply eat it. Portland International Airport, Oregon, has trialled herds of goats, for this purpose, while Chicago O'Hare, Illinois, has teamed up with a nearby animal rescue centre to use goats, sheep, llamas, burros and alpacas to tackle some of the dense vegetation that grows around the airport. This is also a much more eco-friendly method than toxic herbicides. Unfortunately the goats in Portland, they were easy prey for local coyotes, and thus came a need for bodyguards. These came in the form of llamas – apparently coyotes don't like llamas.

Dogs are a common sight at airports in security roles, sniffing out drugs, explosives or any number of other forms of contraband, and passengers are warned not to interact with or distract these dogs. Their use in security areas increased rapidly after 1974 when an NYPD-owned German shepherd sniffed out a bomb inside an aircraft at New York's John F. Kennedy Airport, no doubt saving many lives in the process. There are, however, other roles that dogs perform where interaction is positively encouraged. With names like the Canine Crew, the Pre-Board Pals or the Wag Brigade, some airports have provided therapy dogs to nervous fliers. The idea started after 9/11 at Norman Y. Mineta San Jose International Airport in California and quickly spread around the world. Dogs of all shapes and sizes can be found strolling the likes of Aberdeen (the UK's first airport to implement this programme) and Southampton airports in the UK. This type of programme can also be found in Canada at Toronto, Vancouver and Calgary, a number of US hubs including Pittsburgh and Phoenix, as well as many more, I am sure.

Some of the 'Pre-Board Pals' at Calgary International Airport. (Credit YYC Calgary International Airport)

Wearing vests sporting the words 'stroke me' and the like, more and more major airports are using volunteer therapy dogs as a way of helping stressed passengers.

It's not only dogs that are employed in this role, though. San Francisco Airport has LiLou, a therapy pig, while cats are employed at Denver and Calgary. Whilst over at Cincinnati/Northern Kentucky International Airport, there are miniature horses in the terminal.

Believe it or not, Louis Armstrong New Orleans International Airport has even placed baby alligators in baggage claim areas and passengers are encouraged to pose for a selfie with it. I'm not sure how that goes to calming peoples' nerves though? Soon it might be possible for dogs to be used to provide a non-invasive way of screening passengers for diseases in a similar way to that used for explosives and contraband after early trials showed that dogs could be trained to detect malaria-infected people by their odour with a credible degree of accuracy.

Ever sat next to an animal on board your flight? Setting aside the myriad of stories from developing countries of chickens and goats travelling with their owners in creaking vintage aircraft, there are many animals travelling though airports both legally and not so. Did you know that there are quite a few airlines that allow pets on board including Air Canada, Air France, Lufthansa, Delta and Turkish Airlines. Some of these airlines allow pets of a certain size and weight, others dictate that they must be 'assistance animals', although some people can seem to choose interesting animals to give them assistance. A peacock was purchased a seat on a United flight, despite the owner being told that it could not fly on the aircraft. Possibly even more strange was the case of the emotional support squirrel that was escorted off a Frontier Airlines flight along with its owner, despite claims that clearance had been given by the airline. Often, the rules are led by the area the airline comes from, and in the Middle East, falcons are important to the culture of the United Arab Emirates. The sight of falcons in the cabin is not uncommon and even welcomed by Emirates Airlines – you might even see them flying freely around the cabin!

Animal bird scaring at Ibiza.

However, if you cannot bring your pet on board with you and can't bear the thought of it going in the hold, even though they are in heated, pressurised and well-lit sections, then your only option, if you must fly, is to fly private and employ another of the lesser-known airport companies. Those that deal with pets on aircraft. The list of animal types that have been transported on private jets is almost limitless, but it is mostly dogs, cats and (perhaps surprisingly) ferrets. There are some more unusual travellers, however, for instance a customer who liked to have fresh goat's milk on tap, brought his goat with him, along with a pet nanny whose job it was to look after it and milk the animal, as necessary. For those with the money to do this, the perks for their animals are almost as endless, including anything from ensuring that the correct brand of dietary gourmet pet food or flavour to confirming that the pet's seat is correctly set up for flight, both in comfort and regulatory terms. Inflight puppy massages, grooming, real grass turf for poop and boxes specifically designed for peeing into are some of the other luxuries that pampered pets expect.

In general, there are two sorts of companies that deal with animals on aircraft – those that look after pets almost exclusively, and animal centres that deal with the import and export of animals such as racehorses. These often travel through very specialist centres such as Liege and to a much lesser extent at Milan Malpensa.

These organisations also care for the many different species confiscated from smugglers attempting to get them in or out of a country; in this scenario, temporary accommodation is often provided,

Equine transit facility at Milan Malpensa.

Olly, the one-eared door keeper, was adopted by staff at Olympic House, an office block at Manchester Airport.

A bmibaby 737-300 *Olly Cat Baby*. (Spencer Bennett)

particularly after confiscation by Border Force/Customs. At London Heathrow Animal Reception Centre about 22,000 dogs and cats, 400 horses, 100,000 reptiles, 1,000 birds and 28 million fish are looked after during transit or importation through Heathrow Airport each year, via pet travel schemes or animal shipments. On average, 120 pets are processed daily, although the vast majority of these will travel in the aircraft's hold.

The animals that are smuggled can be just as varied: Liverpool John Lennon Airport reported a passenger trying to smuggle 'a bag of ferrets'; a man in China attempted to smuggle a turtle through security by smearing it in mayonnaise and placing it in a burger bun inside a KFC sandwich box; in Brazil, there was a discovery of 1,000 live spiders inside two suitcases; a Dutchman was caught having sewed hummingbirds into his underwear; and in Bangkok, one man had suitcases full of baby leopards, panthers, monkeys and, wait for it, a bear!

Then there are simply those creatures that have decided to take up residence at an airport. This is exactly what a one-eared ginger cat did at Manchester Airport's main office block, Olympic House. Adopted by staff, the cat was named Olly and lived for several years in a shelter built by staff between terminals One and Three. Capturing the public's imagination, she not only had a dedicated Facebook page with 2,500 friends, there was even an aircraft named after her. When Olly passed away from pneumonia in 2016, a memorial plaque was installed at the airport.

Chapter 11

The Turnaround

'The turnaround can be loosely described as the time between an aircraft arriving and then departing again to a new destination. In an industry where time sensitivity is prevalent, if you get it wrong there can be many consequences. First of all, your passengers will be, at the very least, unimpressed, particularly as airport seating is not generally the most comfortable. Plus, there may be financial implications for the airline, with the airport charging a fee if the aircraft is on the parking stand for longer than it should be, and if the flight is delayed a considerable amount of time then compensation may also be due to the customer.

Who is involved in this intricate dance of people and vehicles that swarm around an aircraft when it arrives gate, or while you are still checking in and watching your bag disappear into the labyrinth below to be sorted scanned and loaded into containers or onto trucks? The first interaction an aircraft might have with people on the ground may well be one that you don't see, as it could be a 'Follow Me' vehicle

Fully automated baggage-sorting system.

This is where your bags disappear after check in.

Follow Me vehicle at Milan Linate.

Above left: Safedock interface unit.

Above right: Safedock scanning unit and display.

(mentioned earlier) guiding it to its parking stand. More often, however, the flight crew will follow a yellow line containing green lights on the taxiways determined by ATC. Once the aircraft arrives at its designated gate, it must stop in exactly the right place to ensure the airbridge (if used) can connect with the door and also to ensure the wings of the aircraft do not hit any structure. To do this, most modern airports now use a system called the Safedock Advanced Visual Docking Guidance Systems, which provides active guidance to pilots, enabling them to park the aircraft themselves. These systems can be integrated with airport and airline systems, to update flight information such as arrival time, the scheduled aircraft type and adjacent gate rules, or the aircraft type.

During the docking process, the technology actively scans the gate area both vertically and horizontally to discriminate between aircraft types and subtypes and then to capture, track and guide the aircraft to its parking spot. At smaller airports or at stands that do not have the technology, the Ops staff help to manually park the aircraft exactly where needed. Although an aircraft may be in position, that doesn't mean all the waiting personnel can start their jobs. Ever wondered what the flashing red light(s) on the fuselage of an aircraft are for? They are called anti-collision lights, which first and foremost are there to improve visibility to others, as well as to act, as the name suggests, as collision avoidance measures by warning other pilots. However, they have another role and that is to warn ground staff and other aircraft that an engine is starting up, running or shutting down, or that the aircraft is about to start moving, and therefore this informs the ground staff the aircraft is not yet

Icelandair 757 using Safedock system.

Marshalling an aircraft onto a stand.

Markings determining where various aircraft types should stop.

safe to approach. So, if you have ever been sitting on an aircraft and wondered why everybody outside appears to be just waiting, it's because your captain or first officer has yet to switch off these lights.

Once the lights are off, various people spring into action. Each airline will have what is known as a nominated handling agent who coordinates the myriad of tasks performed during a turnaround, some of which will are subcontracted to other more specialised organisations.

While the airbridge or stairs are being positioned to allow passengers to disembark, chocks will have been put around the wheels to stop the aircraft from rolling should the parking brake fail. Ground

An Emirates A380 in the process of being turned around.

Ground staff placing chocks under wheels.

power will almost certainly have been attached. Most major airports will have a central source for this, and in essence this will mean that the aircraft will simply be plugged into the mains! Some airports may still use what are basically mobile generators powered by diesel engines to provide power to the aircraft, or if that is not available, airliners have an Auxiliary Power Unit (APU) mounted near the tail, which is able to supply power to some aircraft systems. If you ever hear the noise of an engine coming from an aircraft when boarding, an APU is generally to blame.

At the same time we are getting off our flight, so are our bags. Baggage handlers will be removing the bags from the hold beneath our seats either in bulk within the ULD containers or one at a time, with a mobile conveyor positioned next to the cargo door leading down to carts waiting to be filled up. They will then be pulled by tug to the baggage hall to be unloaded again onto the conveyor belts entering the baggage claim hall or, if in transit, loaded into its onward container. As I mentioned in the cargo chapter, there may also be freight in the belly hold area of passenger aircraft, and this will be removed and possibly replaced with more for the outbound destination.

When the passengers are all off, the cleaning and replenishing of supplies can begin. The speed of the cleaning will depend on the size of aircraft and the type of airline involved. Low-cost airlines have changed the way aircraft are turned around, in order to get the aircraft back in the air in the shortest possible amount of time at the least cost, so, rather than pay for cleaners as other airlines may do, they utilise the cabin crew to clean the aircraft. Cabin crew are also charged with making sure the

Direct power supply unit.

A diesel-powered ground power unit on a remote stand at Cologne-Bonn.

ULD containers with baggage being removed.

Transfer baggage being loaded into containers.

safety cards are in place, flight seats are correctly positioned, and the seat belts are in that familiar crossed position. There are many other tasks to do with ensuring the safety of the aircraft ranging from checking safety equipment to ensuring the aircraft's toilet tank is emptied if required. Did you know an aircraft may well have to divert if the toilets become unusable? During a day spent with One low-cost airline, I was told that the cabin crew had exactly eight minutes to get the cabin clean and ready from the last passenger leaving the aircraft until the first passenger is expected to get on. In contrast, an A380, typically only used by larger airlines, might need a crew of 24 taking 45 minutes to get the aircraft in a fit state for its next load of passengers.

The aircraft also needs to be topped up with supplies from scratch cards to food and Duty Free items. This again is very much dependent on the type of airline and what is offered on board. One of the major items to be replenished is the on-board catering items. Not only the food, but with full service airlines there will be the crockery, glassware and cutlery as well. These and many other items will be delivered by hi-lift vehicles, utilising the doors not attached to stairs or an airbridge. These are the vehicles you see where the whole of the rear section is lifted up by a scissor-style hydraulic unit once the vehicle has been driven into place. These same vehicles will also remove used catering and Duty Free units and often the rubbish from the aircraft.

In-flight catering is food production on a massive scale, where preparation areas are separated into the following sections: hot, cold, vegetables, desserts and for different religious or dietary needs. Each

easyJet allows just eight minutes from last passenger off to first passenger on.

Hi-lift vehicles delivering food and other products for the upcoming flight.

A hi-lift vehicle.

Aircraft being refuelled via bowser.

Refuelling via hydrant and a refuelling vehicle.

meal must be produced and then assembled in a temperature-maintained environment and then rapid chilled before being put into the airline carts in the right numbers and then placed into the hi-lift vehicles. This must all happen within time frame of 45 minutes from kitchen to aircraft.

It's not just passengers that need feeding, however, so do aircraft. Fuel bowsers[7] are historically used to fill up an aircraft's tanks and are still regularly in use. Nowadays, many major airports also have what they call 'fuel farms', generally located close to the airport, feeding into a hydrant system running right through the majority of the parking stands. However, it's not like filling up your car. There is a requirement for a vehicle to link the hydrant to the aircraft, separating any water from the fuel that may be present and filtering and measuring the volume before it flows through a second hose connected to the aircraft, which on commercial aircraft is most often under the wing to ease access.

You may well see one of the many people in hi vis jackets going in and out of the cockpit. This person is more than likely an aircraft dispatcher or turnaround manager. Their job is to co-ordinate all activities on the ground at an airport to ensure the safe, quick and efficient turnaround of aircraft from when they land to the time they depart. This role involves ensuring that tasks, such as cleaning, refuelling and loading are completed on time. A document called the load sheet must be produced, which requires the calculation of how much fuel is required for the payload (weight of passengers, luggage, cargo and the fuel itself) of the aircraft and distance of the journey, amongst many other things. This document will also inform where bags and cargo are loaded in the aircraft so as to maintain an optimum centre of gravity for the aircraft. It may even be the turnaround manager's role to marshall the aircraft onto its stand.

7　A tanker truck that holds aircraft fuel.

Flight crew do not just stay in the cockpit during these activities; one of their jobs is to do a walk around the outside of the aircraft checking for visible defects. Which of the flight crew does this it very much depends on the weather. As one first officer once jokingly told me, 'I can assure you that when it's hammering it down with rain, you can guarantee that I will be doing the walk around!'

A rather unpopular role is that of draining the waste from lavatories, in which a specific vehicle first drains into its tank and then flushes and disinfects the aircraft tank using a separate pipe.

If your trip is through an airport where it is icy, then you may see yet another vehicle around your aircraft. Ice on the wings and other aerodynamic surfaces can lead to a dangerous situation, and therefore you may see heated de-icing fluid being sprayed onto the surfaces just before the aircraft pushes back. At airports where there are regular delays during taxiing, mixed with icing conditions, then aircraft often taxi through automated devices closer to the runway, as the effects of the fluid can be lessened should the aircraft spend too much time on the ground after being de-iced.

Once all checks and processes are complete and passengers are onboard, push back is next, and this can be done with a number of different vehicles called tugs. Older tugs connect to the aircraft nose wheel using a towbar and are nearly always unique to specific types of aircraft. The next generation of tugs, however, position around the nose wheel, then hydraulically lift the nose wheel, or are winched

onto a low base on the tug. This is generally quicker and more efficient, as there is no need for the connection and disconnection and they are not aircraft specific. These are both diesel and electrically powered. In a further development, there are now units like developed by the brand Mototok, which do not require the driver to actually be in the vehicle. They are operated via a handheld unit similar to a computer game console. After push back is complete, the tug driver or dispatcher will hold up the pin used to allow a tug to steer the aircraft, showing the flight crew that cabin crew now have control. When you are finally pushing back for your journey, might I suggest, particularly if you are in Japan or South Korea, that you take a look out of the window. There is

Captain checks the undercarriage during a walkaround.

An A380 being de-iced at the gate.

De-icing vehicle at Milan Airport.

Above and below: Often referred to as 'Lobster' tugs, these units hydraulically lift the nose wheel or are winched onto a low base.

Tug attached to an A320 via a towbar.

Mototok unit being operated to push back a British Airways A320.

a very good chance that you will see a good selection of all the people involved in the turnaround either bowing or waving at you.

As you can see, there is a massive amount of work to be done by a small army of men and women from many different organisations. This work needs to be done within a prescribed timescale, meaning there are lots of jobs that need to be done concurrently. On top of that, the sheer size of the area being worked on must also be appreciated – the footprint of an A380 stand alone is very similar to a large football ground such as Manchester United's Old Trafford.

Thumbs up and confirmation of pin removal.

Chapter 12

Signs, Lines and Machines

During taxiing, you may notice that there are signs directing aircraft and airport staff around the airfield. Then there are the weird and wonderful looking constructions dotted around the runways. What comes next will hopefully shed a little light onto what the signs mean and just what those pieces of metal are.

Airfield signs can be freestanding units, either painted or light boxes. Signs can also be painted on the runways, taxiways and apron areas. There are six basic types of sign: mandatory, location, direction, destination, information and runway distance remaining. Many will be found grouped together. Most are permanent, some are temporary. The mandatory signs are always white markings/lettering on a red background. These signs are used to protect critical areas such as runway entrance points and ILS-critical areas, and include things as simple as a no entry sign.

Reykjavik Airport windsock and runway designator sign.

Entrance to runway 14 left at Cologne-Bonn showing the runway threshold.

Above: Numerous airfield signs at Manchester.

Left: Temporary stop signs used for works.

Mandatory sign detailing runway designations and Instrument landing system (ILS) category.

Location signs have yellow markings/lettering on a black background and identify a taxiway, holding point or a runway on which an aircraft is located. The runway signs are particularly useful when runways are in close proximity each other and are there to reduce possible confusion.

Directional and destination signs are both black markings/lettering on a yellow background and include arrows pointing towards another area, be that a runway or a taxiway.

'N5' is the location sign in this grouping, in between two directional signs.

Destination signs direct aircraft towards different areas of an airfield such as specific aprons, terminals, FBOs, military areas or even a selection of stands. In fact, the stand numbers on the terminal may also be of the same design.

The apron markings also consist of mainly yellow and black, although as can be seen in this picture on page 115 of the closed Nicosia Airport – left just as it was when closed in 1974 after the Turkish invasion of Cyprus – this has not always been the case. The apron markings showing the stand numbers are in white.

Today, the vehicle road systems around airports are also in white.

This grouping is mainly directional signs, with the exception of the 'C', which is the taxiway location.

A directional sign indicating the destination of a military ramp.

Stand 4 and the abandoned terminal at Nicosia International Airport in the UN buffer zone between south and north Cyprus.

Runway markings are in addition to these. Each landing strip is actually two runways identified by 60ft tall and 20ft wide white numbers that correspond to the magnetic direction or heading of the runway, rounded off to the nearest 10 degrees. The runway name is pronounced with each digit separately. If there are two parallel runways, there is an additional 'L' for left or 'R' for right, with a 'C' for centre if there is a third. For example, at London Heathrow, the two parallel runways face 272 degrees at one end and 092 degrees at the other. This means that they are identified as 27L/09R and 27R/09L. These are called runway designators. In the US, they drop the initial '0', however.

The amount of further markings depend on the category of the airfield the runway serves. All runways require a white-striped centreline as well as the designator. After that, other markings to signify the threshold (and indeed what is called a displaced threshold), aiming point, touchdown zone and edge markings. The threshold marking identifies the beginning of the runway and consists of a white bar to signify the beginning of the runway, if required. Then there are a number of longitudinal white stripes arranged evenly at each side of the centreline. The number of stripes indicate the width of the runway. A displaced threshold is where a portion of runway is usable for taxi, take-off, and roll-out but not for landing. If this is permanent, it is marked with white arrows on the centre. There are other markings involving chevrons in white to signify a temporary condition, crosses to indicate areas not fit for aircraft movement and yellow chevrons only fit for use in an emergency landing.

Road markings at Milan/Bergamo.

Runway 23R designator sign at Manchester.

Graphic showing runway markings.

Ariel view of runway 34R at Doha.

Aerial view of runway 25 at Woodford, showing the displaced threshold.

Runway aiming points on runway 07/25 at Townsville, Australia.

For runways over 2,400 metres (7,875ft), aiming point markings are placed 400 metres (1,300ft) from the runway threshold. This distance is reduced for shorter runways. They are represented as a pair of large white rectangles, giving pilots a visual guidance to where they should be touching down. Touchdown zone markings identify the area on which aircraft should land and consist of groups of one, two, and three rectangular bars, evenly arranged in pairs along the runway centre line. Spaced in 150-metre (500ft) increments, they provide distance information for the remaining available landing length. Edge markings are a simple solid white line delineating between the runway and what is beyond.

Airport lighting is used to mark the way, and as a traffic light system, for example red stop bars (a number of red lights across a taxiway) tell aircraft to stop. I would also like to mention the two alternately flashing amber lights at each side of a runways that signal holding positions, simply because they are called Wig-Wags.

The windsock not only tells air crew in which direction the wind is blowing and indicates its speed. Each orange or white stripe represents an estimated three knots of wind speed, and when horizontal and fully extended, it suggests a wind speed of at least 15 knots. A more accurate instrument to measure wind speed and direction is called an anemometer, and there will be multiples of these units close to runway aiming points.

Above: A red stop bar is visible under this Turkish A321.

Left: Wig-Wags are positioned each side of all runway holding positions.

Windsock and ultrasonic anemometer.

There are many other aerial arrays and other, almost unworldly, items dotted around airfields. They are mainly seen in proximity to the runways, as their roles are most often inextricably linked to guide aircraft to an airport. Some of these items include:

- Distance-measuring equipment (DME)

Most often coupled with a VHF Omnidirectional Range (VOR) system, these units calculate an aircraft's flight position from the transmitter and then displays this to the flight crew. This distance

The metal tower in this photo is an NDB, or non-directional beacon, that simply transmits a signal that an aircraft can use to find its location. The Distance Measuring Equipment (DME) is housed in the checkered building.

Manchester Airport's Doppler VHF Omnidirectional Range (DVOR), including DME.

is called the 'slant range', which is the line-of-sight distance between the aircraft and the DME transmitter.

- VHF Omnidirectional Range (VOR)

These can sometimes be known as DVORs with the addition of the word 'Doppler'. A DVOR is a short/medium-range radio navigation system that aids in calculating an aircraft's flight position and direction in relation to its destination using VHF signals between 108.00 to 117.95 MHz sent from a radio beacon. In the main, VORs and DVORs also have a DME co-located.

- Instrument Landing System (ILS)

This is a ground-based radio navigation system that gives pilots lateral and vertical guidance towards the runway and can be used to automatically land aircraft in bad weather. An ILS is made up of two parts. The localiser, which is a fence of red and white prongs, is responsible for guiding the aircraft laterally, and the glideslope emitter, which is a tower with three oblong boxes, provides the vertical guidance. Therefore, when used together, the aircraft's systems or the pilot can guide the aircraft down onto the runway. The bottom picture overleaf shows the red and white glideslope unit in the foreground, with the older style of cup and vane anemometer to the rear. The DME can often form part of the ILS array. The categories of ILS are CAT l, CAT ll and CAT lllA/B/C. To describe the differences in these categories in detail is outside of the scope of this book. In short, the category of landing any aircraft can undertake is based on equipment the airport has and the local visibility, the ceiling height and what is known as the Runway Visual Range (RVR), alongside the level of training/qualification

Above: An A320 passing over an ILS localiser.

Left: The red and white glideslope unit is in the foreground with the older style of cup and vane anemometer behind.

05L
GP

A vast range of equipment helps an aircraft land, even in zero visibility.

Precision Approach Path Indicators (PAPIs) on runway 36 at Milan Linate.

a pilot has. An aircraft can actually land automatically when in CAT lll conditions, even with zero visibility. However, low-visibility landings often will not be undertaken as the crew may find it difficult to get to their allotted stand. Even worse, should some mishap come to the aircraft, then the emergency services may have difficulty finding the aircraft. This is something that the fire service in Genoa fell foul of back in 2004, when a Britannia 757 aircraft with a full emergency, landed in low visibility. Torrential rain and a failure of runway lighting reduced visibility so much so that the aircraft wasn't found by the fire service for over 18 minutes.

- Precision Approach Path Indicators (PAPI) and APAPI (an Abbreviated version).

PAPIs are a visual landing aid and consist of four (two for APAPI) lights in a row, which either show red or white, depending on an aircraft's height in relation to the runway.

- Visual Approach Slope Indicators (VASI)

These work on the same principle as PAPI, but the lights are split into two sets of two, one set above the other.

- Runway Visual Range (RVR)

As mentioned earlier, RVR shows the visibility at set points on a runway, normally touchdown, midpoint and runway end. These items are critical in determining what ILS category of landing

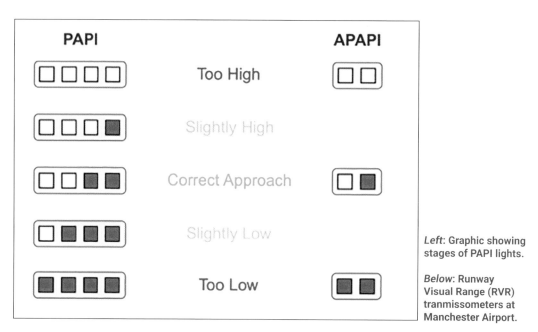

PAPI / APAPI

PAPI		APAPI
☐☐☐☐	Too High	☐☐
☐☐☐■	Slightly High	
☐☐■■	Correct Approach	☐■
☐■■■	Slightly Low	
■■■■	Too Low	■■

Left: Graphic showing stages of PAPI lights.

Below: Runway Visual Range (RVR) tranmissometers at Manchester Airport.

is possible. In simple terms, these are made up of two units called transmissometers. Between them, they measure the density of particles in the air, such as water droplets, snow or even dust that passes between the two sensor elements, which then is translated into a usable RVR measurement.

RVR transmissometers measure the density of particles in the air.

There will also be the actual radar devices spinning away on the top of buildings or towers, such as these, in the picture below, at Manchester Airport that are the primary and secondary surveillance radars on the left tower, with the surface movement radar 'seeing' what is on the ground at an airport on the right.

The jobs that I have covered, and the people that perform them, are but a few of those that keep an airport running. There are many more – more than I can put into just one book, and I apologise to those missed out. However, I hope this has given you a little insight into the world of an airport as well as providing some entertainment. To you, my reader, many thanks for taking the time to read this book. I really hope you enjoyed reading it as much as I did writing it.

Safety in operations comes from a multitude of sources. This picture also shows an anemometer and glideslope emitter, in addition to a set of PAPIs next to the runway.

Other books you might like:

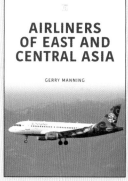

AIRLINERS OF EAST AND CENTRAL ASIA

GERRY MANNING

Modern Commercial Aircraft
Series, Vol. 1

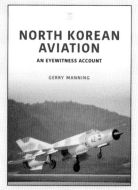

NORTH KOREAN AVIATION

AN EYEWITNESS ACCOUNT

GERRY MANNING

AIRLINERS OF THE 2000s

GERRY MANNING

Historic Commercial Aircraft
Series, Vol. 5

JET

THE ENGINE THAT CHANGED THE WORLD

GRAHAM HOYLAND

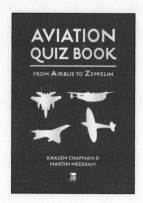

AVIATION QUIZ BOOK

FROM AIRBUS TO ZEPPELIN

KHALEM CHAPMAN &
MARTIN NEEDHAM

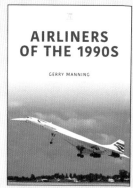

AIRLINERS OF THE 1990S

GERRY MANNING

Historic Commercial
Aircraft Series, Vol. 4

For our full range of titles please visit:
shop.keypublishing.com/books

VIP Book Club
Sign up today and receive
TWO FREE E-BOOKS

Be the first to find out about our forthcoming
book releases and receive exclusive offers.

Register now at keypublishing.com/vip-book-club

Our VIP Book Club is a 100% spam-free zone, and we will never share your email with anyone else.
You can read our full privacy policy at: privacy.keypublishing.com